D1597131

Unearthing

Alan Moore | Mitch Jenkins

begin the

Disappea

Dis-
co-
nnect-
ing

all the visual cues that advertise the presence of a mind, a self that's
here somewhere, already hidden. One way this may be accomplished,
a technique he's previously playground bully-tested, is by standing still,
ideally in some liminal location, in some threshold area, sheltering wall
that edged the schoolyard, cavern, hilltop, city limit, spaces between
world and underworld, skyline and sky, streetlights and wilderness. Don't
move. For almost sixty years

do n ' t move.

Stand still and turn to urban furniture, to your own monument, to
landscape. Bypass all the cultural motion sensors, become sub-or
supra-liminal, white noise on the surveillance footage.

In the country of the blind the one-eyed man is king, and, better yet,

invisible.

Steve Moore sat in the armchair opposite his bed with ballpoint pen and notepad, spiral
bound,
neat sloping capitals, each line a blue queue leaning forward, barely masking their
impatience, as the book-crammed room around him pales unnoticed into
dusk there on the top of Shooters Hill.

MAN WITH A

foolish

grin,

PERFECTLY STILL,

as failing light
adjusts to match his ash-slide hair, to match the
wet-slate gleam his skin has, the South London
moontan.

Slowly, the defining edge is lost in grey on grey,
a photo undeveloping

THE TEXTURES VANISH IN OBLITERATING GLOSS, DETAIL

Fine wrinkles spreading from the corners of his eyes,
CURVED UP AROUND THE BRO
curved down around the cheekbon

All this erased and then the body outline fades, the slight frame tł
conspires with posture to seem even slighter, basically an Adam's apple a
its support system, melted, gone into the darkening of the cosy room, t
manhutch with its pagan icon huddle. Finally the only light is this of t
metropolis, the great black garden of a million flowers on fire spread supi
and magnificent below his rear, north-facing bedroom window.

THIS AND

M O O N

XCUSE THEMSELVES.

—— FACE LIKE A MAGNETIC FIELD.

LIGHT

Black on silver-dusted black the hill pokes up its positive yang terminal into the night's electrolyte, plated across the centuries with urban dream in a metallic rind. Seabed before the ice age, residues of fossil night-sweat crown the tumulus, a cradle-cap of gravel sheltering the clay and chalk beneath while all around wore down to lowland, marine aeons half-remembered still in seaside decors that incongruously dot the closes and steep lanes. Its sickle-shaped mass crystal-shot with *Selenites Rhomboidalis,*

Shooters Hill is

dreaming London, dreaming

London: up:

low on its northern slope a chalk fault that collapsed creating the Thames valley, gouging out a life-sump for the Neolithic swill to fill, the pallid Morlock scrum, chalk-mining chavs blowing their barter on bone bling in settlements at Plumstead, Woolwich, barnacled below the sleeping hill's north flank. Part of a queasy hypnagogic swirl erupting from its moonstone synapses the Stone Age shacks and faces flow like liquid, an accelerated morph seen from its geological perspective, turning into Bronze Age fishing villages and Trinovante squints.

Riff-raff gets buried under middling heaps at Blackheath, kings and chieftains in great mounds up on the hilltop, sacred bulges on the hunched horizon. Five of these were flattened when they built the Laing Estate in the late 1930s but still one remains, a railed-off and grassed-over hump there at the junction of Plum Lane and Brinklow Crescent, sole surviving god of Shooters Hill and also dreaming, underneath the yellow weeds. Down on the far side is the boundary where the dream ends. Kent begins, and London disappears.

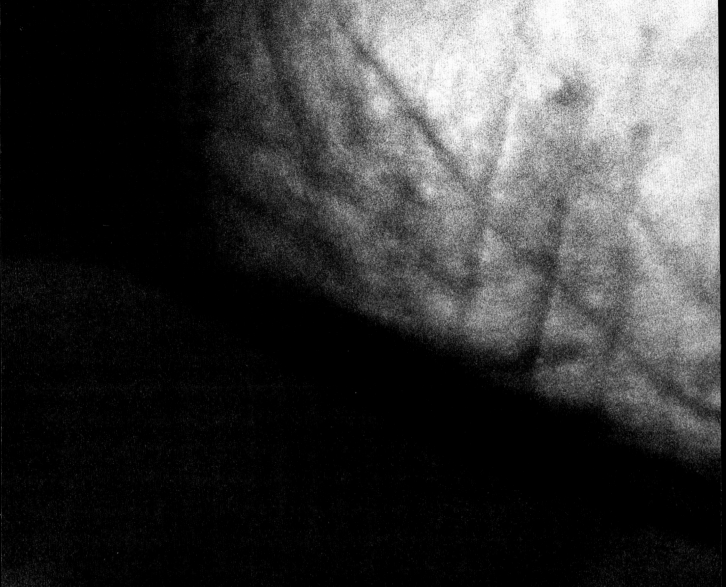

Back in the bedroom of the house where he's lived all his life, Steve Moore lies facing shelves of *I Ching* reference volumes, fast asleep on his right side so as to soothe that faltering gurgle in the ventricles, not half a dozen paces from the spot where he was born. Close to his face, upon a book-bare ledge stands framed the gem-like miniature he painted during April 1989, a portrait of Selene, Greek moon-goddess, moon herself, naked and white, the sable-stippled cunt, the eyes and lips that seem to move beneath the glass fogged by a silvery aerosol, his every night-breath. There beside the picture rests the notepad and the ballpoint pen. Waking to dark or dawn's stone-blue he'll scrawl his dreams down, key words, phrases, image-prompts for later when they'll be typed up in full and added to the ring-bound stack, the log of an alternate life meticulously kept for more than thirty years with earlier entries dating from his childhood, messages from otherworldly scientists with winsome daughters on the planet Uniceptor IV.

Faint tremors in balloon-thin eyelid skin betray the alien jostle taking place below, the nightlife. Skimming frictionless, his shoe-soles half an inch above the paving slabs, he slips through lamp-lit streets, disturbing analogues of those he grew amongst, walks to this day. To lift the plain black cover of a dream-file is to fretfully peel back a rectangle of tarmac from the skin of the locale, exposing a new stratum, laying bare a shadow neighbourhood beneath and making audible the creepy chat of shadow neighbours, ghost-train gossip, twilight ideologies.

He dreams the hill with different weather and new cellars. Giant roses hanging in the night sky over Plumstead or pellucid covered markets under Blackheath. The unnerving day-deserted cul-de-sacs and the eight-thousand-year-old woodlands just across the humming road become the sets of strange pre-title sequences for lost *Avengers* episodes. Diana Rigg, dead relatives and Hong Kong action movie stars move purposeful and sinister through semi-detached situations under lead skies. Elevator doors shrug shut before the lift slides sideways through unfathomable offices. Loveable horrors squirming in the garden pond. He takes a shit on the top deck of a four-eighty-six bus labouring towards the

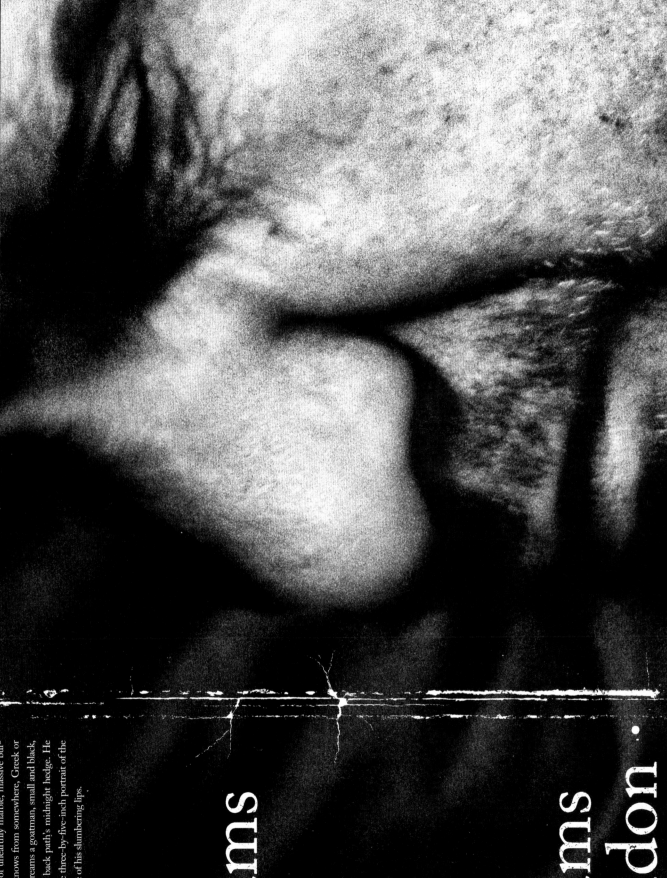

crest, sees roadside excavations of unearthly marble, massive buried architectures in a style he knows from somewhere, Greek or Babylonian Art Nouveau. He dreams a goatman, small and black, lounging insouciantly atop the back path's midnight hedge. He dreams his room, he dreams the three-by-five-inch portrait of the goddess within misting distance of his slumbering lips.

He dreams the hill. The hill dreams London.

Arced across its crown is Watling Street,
is Shooters Hill Road,
the old Dover Road,
along which channel the transforming energies
leak in, foam downhill to engulf the capital.

JULIUS CAESAR'S

BRIEF EXPLORATORY SORTIE DURING

55 BC

had its first sight of the new principality from here,

as did Agricola's more serious invasion force that followed later by almost a century.

The same hushed apprehension of a vast and brilliant counterpane below,

untidily tucked under at the far horizon, messy and unmade,

the river's copper ribbon spooled across it,

crumpling towards the east and settlements like biscuit crumbs.

THE THREE GREAT WOODS, JACK, CASTLE, OXLEAS,

rolling up the hill in black iron wave-fronts, smashing in a pale green spray across the peak and into Kent. Briefly, amidst its breathless fluid tumble of alarming images, the hill hallucinates a filigree of Roman ideology, a loosely outlined golden threadwork stitched half-heartedly into the landscape's quilt, immediately unpicked, unravelled in a pungent woolly tangle of new Saxon place names, Eltham, Charlton, Plumstead, Woolwich, Welling. Sheters Hill?

The road becomes a drovers' track, an overloaded artery to pump the meat and money up, the massive herds a grubby, lousy scarf wound out along its length. The gas-fat crowbait fallen into wayside ditches blurs to grease and blowflies, melts into the rockdream's rush and flicker, the frenetic lantern-show erupting in chalk scribbles, boiling clay, out of a subterrene unconscious, flash-frames in the blacked-out skull theatre of a buried Bronze-Age god.

Jet coral, London is accumulated, squirms and grows in the detached gaze of the vantage. Royal successions in a strobe of ermine. On the cow-track swarming spectres crackle into being and as soon are vanished, blazing specks and filaments scratched white upon the film's emulsion. Out a-Maying with one of his Catherines, Henry the Eighth attends a Robin Hood Fair, Shooters Hill as mediaeval theme park, and meets players dressed as

Robin,
Friar Tuck,
Will Scarlet,
Bashful,
Goofy.

𝕾𝖔𝖔𝖓 𝖙𝖍𝖊𝖗𝖊𝖆𝖋𝖙𝖊𝖗 𝕬𝖓𝖓𝖊 𝖔𝖋 𝕮𝖑𝖊𝖛𝖊𝖘 𝖈𝖗𝖔𝖘𝖘𝖊𝖘 𝖙𝖍𝖊 𝖍𝖎𝖑𝖑 𝖆𝖓𝖉 𝖎𝖘 𝖎𝖒𝖒𝖊𝖉𝖎𝖆𝖙𝖊𝖑𝖞 𝖘𝖊𝖓𝖙 𝖕𝖆𝖈𝖐𝖎𝖓𝖌 𝖇𝖆𝖈𝖐 𝖙𝖍𝖊 𝖘𝖆𝖒𝖊 𝖜𝖆𝖞, 𝖋𝖆𝖎𝖑𝖎𝖓𝖌 𝖙𝖔 𝖑𝖎𝖛𝖊 𝖚𝖕 𝖙𝖔 𝖙𝖍𝖊 𝕳𝖆𝖓𝖘 𝕳𝖔𝖑𝖇𝖊𝖎𝖓 𝕻.𝕽. 𝖕𝖆𝖈𝖐𝖆𝖌𝖊 𝖙𝖍𝖆𝖙 𝖕𝖗𝖊𝖈𝖊𝖉𝖊𝖉 𝖍𝖊𝖗.

Archery ranges smeared across the lower slopes towards the east provide the shooters who will either give the hill its name or else will lend that name a spurious justification and the sixteenth century whistles by, a rattling sideways rain of arrows.

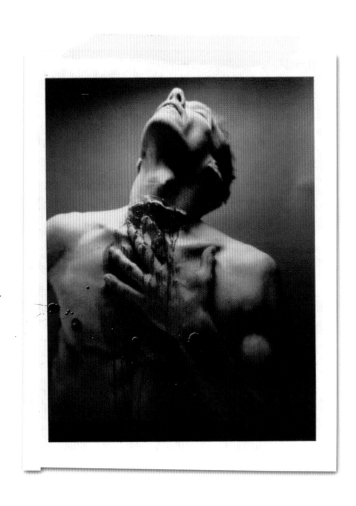

1588

At the ragged edges of Elizabethan London's proto-psychedelic swoon, murderers blossom on the steep road's wooded margins, springing up around the base of the armada beacon raised in 1588, cutpurses ripening to cut-throats, claret splashed across the turnpike and, inevitably, a new nickname.

Hill of Doors

a missing psychotronic flick from Herschel Gordon Lewis, William Castle.

AGENT ORANGE OPTIONS are employed to thin the bandit cover. Come the sixteen hundreds and the shearing of the hill commences, north side gradually reduced to Roundhead stubble. Come the eighteenth century and building starts, the place's fever-visions crystallised to lines and corners, brick growths thrusting through the

SHAVEN

CALP, the coronet materialising one point at a time. First inns arrive, providing watering holes for drovers, boltholes for

THE HIGHWAYMEN,

AND

Holes

IN GENERAL.

Fanny On The Hill, The Catherine Wheel, Sun In The Sands

and then in 1749 the crowning glory of THE BULL, *palatial edifice* erected on the summit with its glittering pleasure gardens, with its wells and fields and stables, its star chef and its extensive cellars.

Sumptuous hostelries and god-like view now make the dreaming hill itself a focal point for human aspirations, human dreams, as inns are followed by the follies, haunts and halls of hubris-sozzled toffs groping towards Olympus. Princess Charlotte dwells at Shrewsbury House, face underlit a ghostly scarab green by bubbling glass retorts, a first stab at extracting gas from coal. A little further down the hillside to the east, in the still-wooded reaches south of Watling Street the widow of Sir William James raises a single-turret castle, Severndroog, **in 1784,**

commemorating her late husband's naval victory over the pirate chieftain Conagee Angria at his Malabar coast sea-fort thirty years before. The tower looms up to peer between the treetops at the city spread below, brass sightlines set into its wooden crows' nest rail aligned with distant London monuments, with neighbouring counties, watching for the brig-and hordes that may one day see the from the backed-up drain of the metropolis, engulf the hill in rum, bum, concertina, cheap accessories. Just up the road, the Lidgbird family are owners of the land on which The Bull is standing, with their stately pile Broom Hall next door and on the right, while at the hill's foot by the gallows and the gibbet-fields are former Neolithic camps accumulating mass and muscle, the Royal Arsenal and Royal Artillery in Woolwich from the kick-off of the eighteenth century. Burned powder notes perfume the nagging westerly, spark flintlock images of plunder, war and revolution in the free-associating stone subconscious, in its perilous, delirious mix.

Always a touchstone of imaginings and point of moonrise for the ancient settlements, their dead kings hulking from its turf, the heap attracts new fictions now. Already a collage of other men's exploits and novelists' inventions the Dick Turpin story is attached to Shooters Hill, the Essex Boy misplaced in a confusion over rumoured hiding places deep in nearby woods. Then at the century's end during the 1790s, Sydney Carton's Dover-bound coach founders in the mudslide up towards the brink, its passengers dismounting terrified on the notorious bloodhill, made hysterically blind to the glaring facade of the Bull Inn, there at the peak for more than forty years by then.

The fictions come, and next the fiction-mongers. During 1800, Wordsworth, barely thirty, has his cottage overlooking Woolwich Common underneath the hill, and as the villas of the middle classes start to fill the spaces between hilltop mansions in the early nineteenth century, Algernon Blackwood's future family home and birthplace buds amongst them. The new residents are prisoners in fairyland, commuters waiting for a train of neon rollergirls to carry them Starlight Express into eternity. They line up at the mounting block, stood knee deep in a fertile scurf of faltered social visions, different fictions, no less wistful. Shooters Hill as healing spa or even enclave hilltop town, as site of a colossal pyramid, titanic mausoleum for the nation's Titan dead. The slowly spreading actual homes and streets, unwittingly, invariably, sink foundations deep into a pre-existent dreamcrust.

Steve
Moore
sleeps
on
wrinkled
bedsheets
made
of
sand
beneath
Silurian
seas.

life sleeps, a rum

ENCYSTED

mass within the 'glacier ice, at cradled in the highest boughs at

PREHISTORIC FOREST

Mumbling, he rolls over into servant quarters in Broom Hall's east wing before the walls dissolve, are realigned into those of the quiet semi he shares with his elder brother, with his goddess, with his books, his work. The closed eyes, closing an account or ... ... his knees and worlds away the woman next door's hall clock chimes another quarter-hour with brisk and brass enthusiasm inappropriate to the drowsing moment. Ageing paper perfumes stew and simmer at the threshold of awareness, and the soft trough between lower lip and front teeth silts with curds of mango pulp, its citrus flinch smoothed into a thick equatorial honey, sweet and rounded as a Gauguin buttock. Everything he is, his biologic destiny, his father's stroke approaching that eighth hole, blood histories, his code embroidered on the pillow's edge in spittle threads.

Back in the 1880s his paternal great-grandfather is in Dublin putting down the Fenians, his granddad born there in the barracks to a mortal term obscure and brief, ended in 1919 with his eldest son, eleven-year-old Arthur James, becoming breadwinner. He never takes to 'Arthur', more a cleared throat than a name, preferring Jim. Hurries to work through Charlton's winter streets, head down, ears aching with the chill and mesmerised by his own schoolboy shoes, their rhythm on the pavement with its suede of frost, unable to believe this is his life, Frederick Boehm's, the company producing paper-size in Belvedere there on the river, just past Plumstead, just past Welling. Panting with the pace he leaves his breath behind him, frozen dragon embryos suspended in the dark and biting air.

More than a decade later, Jim's still with the same firm when their fit new secretary starts, Winifred Mary Deeks, nine years his junior, a tidy little bit of posh from the sedate, disputed borderlands where New Cross bleeds to Lewisham. She can't stand 'Wini-fred', all wisps and webs and spiders in the wedding cake, sticking with Mary. Delicate and lovely, paper in her blood with printers somewhere in the background stir and older brother Francis in Naval Intelligence while younger sibling Donald works his way up through the ranks at Foyle's, ends up as a distributor of academic publications specialising in the Orient. They're stepping out together before long and Jim with his own family tree all guncotton and powder-burns hardly believes his luck. They wed in 1937 and start looking for a place to live, somewhere that's safe and self-contained above the grime and hustle and their eyes drift upwards inexorably towards the hilltop, where the sky fast-forwards into black and the full moon launches itself in ambush from behind the summit, flies up at the throat of night.

They find their des. res. in a muted cul-de-sac just opposite the melancholic front of the Memorial Hospital, erected circa 1920 on the site of the old Admiralty Telegraph where windmill vanes once clacked their urgent semaphore. New house, one of those knocked up in the 'thirties where Broom Hall had stood, a previous owner bolted after eighteen months, no reason given. Jim and Mary take up occupation there in 1938, a perfect fit with the Mrs. Dale's Diary ambience. Peace and quiet, a cousin on the Moore side of the family moved in next door and forest just across the Dover Road, itself barely a murmur. Future stretched secure before them and both of an age where all of this could still turn out to be a song, a Ronald Coleman film, a musical, Darby and Joan who once were Jack and Jill. The hopes and dreams come with the elevation, then, within

a year, SO DOES THE LUFTWAFFE.

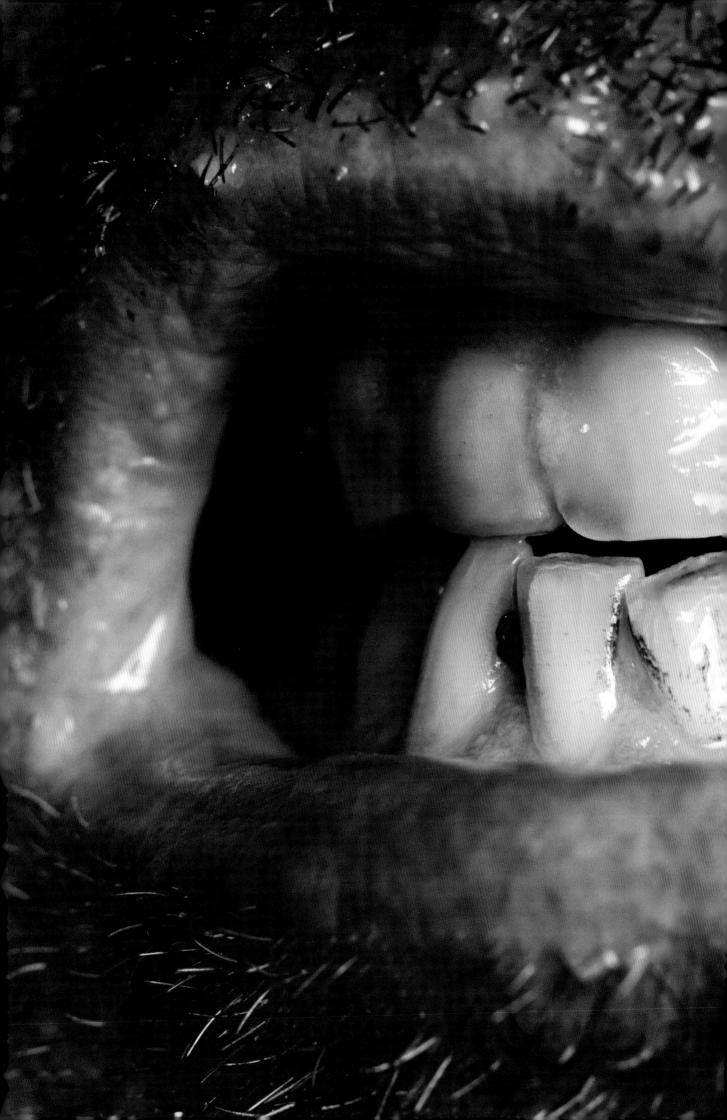

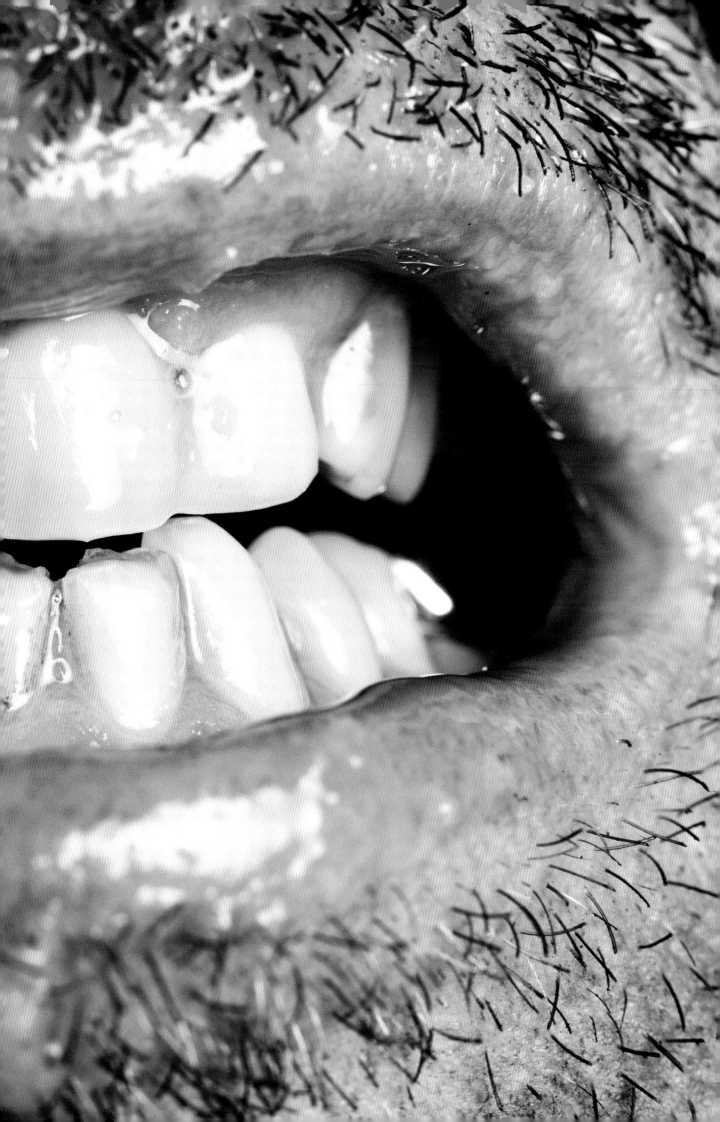

THE ROMAN OBSERVATION POINT
is now the highest land between

Berlin

London

Jim, his father's barrack-room nativity just one twist further down the helical ancestral staircase, mans the rocket battery that's stationed on the golf course, uphill from the former gibbet fields. Phosphorous tracers hyphenating giant blackness, boom and siren, recoil shuddering the green and distant firebursts pluming from the cower of the city. Their sole kill disputed, shared with other guns, the battery claims to have brought down only half a bomber: one-winged like a sycamore pod, just commencing its erratic spiralling descent on London when the rockets hit, the pilot's startled profile clearly visible in the exposed cross-section cockpit, open to an iron wind. Battle of Britain over with, the couple feel they can relax, allow themselves a modest and celebratory drink of future. First son

CHRISTOPHER ARRIVES IN 1943, SPIT OF HIS DAD, THEN 1944 AND V-BOMBS, many of which fail to clear the hill.

British Intelligence is leaking fake reports to Germany of rockets overshooting London, hoping that they'll underestimate instead and hammer Kent rather than W.1. Back on Shot-Over Hill there's charred gaps, sudden spaces in the uniformly 1930s rows where architectural incongruities will one day rise from scorched earth. Shooters Hill becomes a surprise pot of bricks and offal at the far end of gravity's rainbow. Two doors down gets taken out while Jim is bathing. Bathroom ceiling comes down all in one piece, trapping him there in the tub but sparing him the rain of roof and chimney that immediately follows. That could have so easily been that, Mary a single parent, Chris an only child, and all the wave of possibility to come collapsed there into suds and

rubble on the sopping lino.

EVEN WITH THE WAR'S END, understandably, the pair decide to wait and see if there are any more *surprises...*

Nazi flying saucers piloted by Hitler's brain, Fourth Reich mole-machines erupting through the pavem
from the
hollow earth beneath...before they risk another child. Stephen James Moore is born
to a full moon on June 11th, 1949, *a crescent mark staining his*

forearm, there upon the CRESCENT HILL.

GEMINI,
like his brother.

Fire of air, the tarot Knight of Swords, the intellectual faculty in its most pristine and idealised aspect, almost mint condition on account of having been so seldom taken from its box and played with in the human mud. The corresponding tarot trump is number six, The Lovers, the alchemic principle of Solvé, *or analysis. Of separation. Name the baby Stephen with the name deriving from 'stephane', a type of crown unusually favoured by Greek goddesses, most notably their lunar deity. His earliest memory is of September 20th the next year, 1950,*

fifteen months old, held up by his mother to look at a bright blue moon, this famous rarity

occasioned by vast tracts of

forest then ablaze

in
CANADA.

He will remember this for years, but as a dream,
like floating slowly down the stairs into the hallway's umber,
or the skeletal, androgynous old woman, lower face concealed by a bandanna,
who unpeels into malign existence from the wardrobe door,

ABDUCTS HIS HAPLESS TOYS

Time is discrete from space until the eyelids close. He's snoring in the fourth dimension as a gorgeous fractal millipede, his limbs a frilly Muybridge ruff, asleep on Duchamp's staircase.

He's a Julia Set, an emerald gorgon fern unwinding from the luminous coelenterate complexity that is his mother, drifting there beside him in a grand fluid continuum, the albumen contained by spacetime's egg. Jewel-coral, with his tail in the zygotic damp, his head cremated dust scattered across the Brinklow Crescent burial mound, he's a subsidiary offshoot coiling from the parent form, evolving its own crenellated intricacies but forever tied to the maternal Mandelbrot. Moored fast.

Back in the captured heat of his terrestrial bed one leg kicks out, dog-basket reflex, and along the overbody's snaking flank its insectile chaotic trim of arms and legs is rippled by a Tiller Girl convulsion. In suspension, monstrous in a lotus web above eternity,

amid the gem anemones he dreams his life.

The awkward childhood,

raised in low cloud up on the sequestered peak and cringing at the stark immensities about him. The most lightless, smogbound days were called 'black puddings'. Is that dream or memory, that detail? Bawling from day one at nursery, singled out as best friend and primary prey by the four-year-old sexual sadist who, as luck would have it, lives two doors away; is inescapable. With each attempt to integrate himself into the baffling social jigsaw he discovers that his ears and mouth have fists in. Suffers military hazing rituals, punishment beatings, the full Deep Cut treatment, from the Cubs. With nowhere left to go unless he wants a kicking from the Brownies, he removes to the interior, the private bone-walled Wendy House, the great indoors of books and small ventriloquistic wars to annex mantelpiece or carpet, solitary games

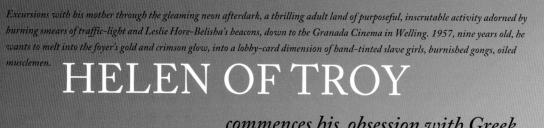

Excursions with his mother through the gleaming neon afterdark, a thrilling adult land of purposeful, inscrutable activity adorned by burning smears of traffic-light and Leslie Hore-Belisha's beacons, down to the Granada Cinema in Welling. 1957, nine years old, he wants to melt into the foyer's gold and crimson glow, into a lobby-card dimension of hand-tinted slave girls, burnished gongs, oiled musclemen.

HELEN OF TROY

commences his obsession with Greek

MYTH,

THE ILIAD READ BY THE AGE OF TEN

and then the hungry grey sponge in his head moves on from gods and legends to soak up the planets and the constellations named for them. Science, history, astronomy and classical mythology. In his retreat from fresh air and its various antagonisms, inadvertently he has become class swot, become more eminently punchable, practically begging for it.

OI, YOU.

YES, YOU.

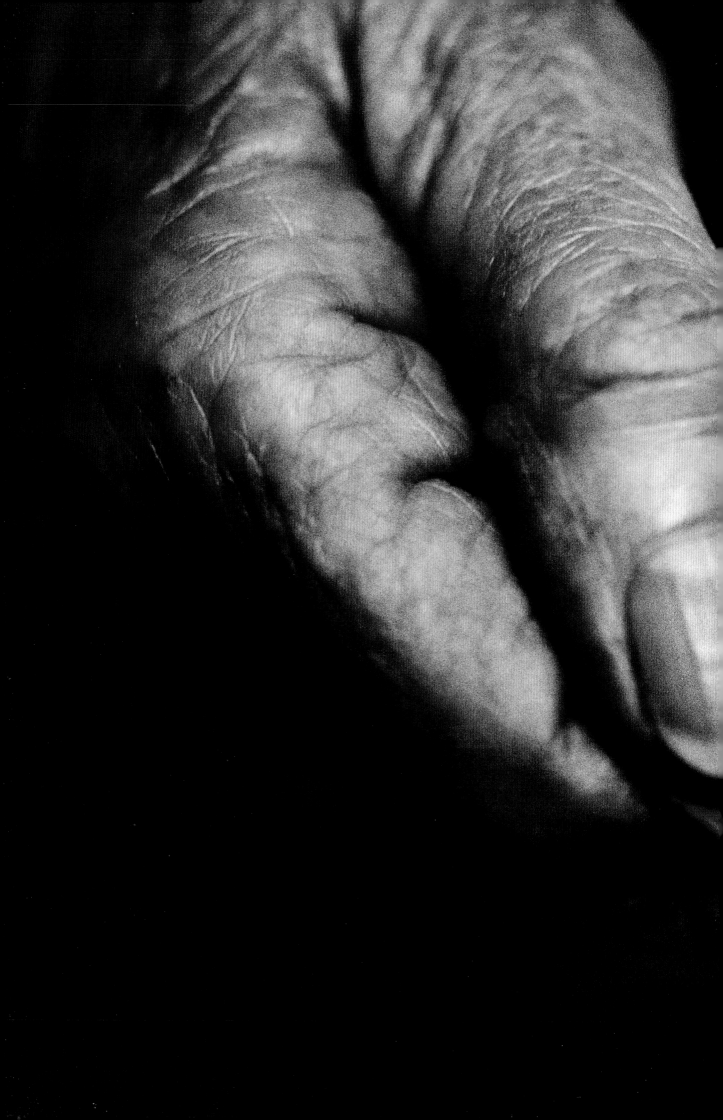

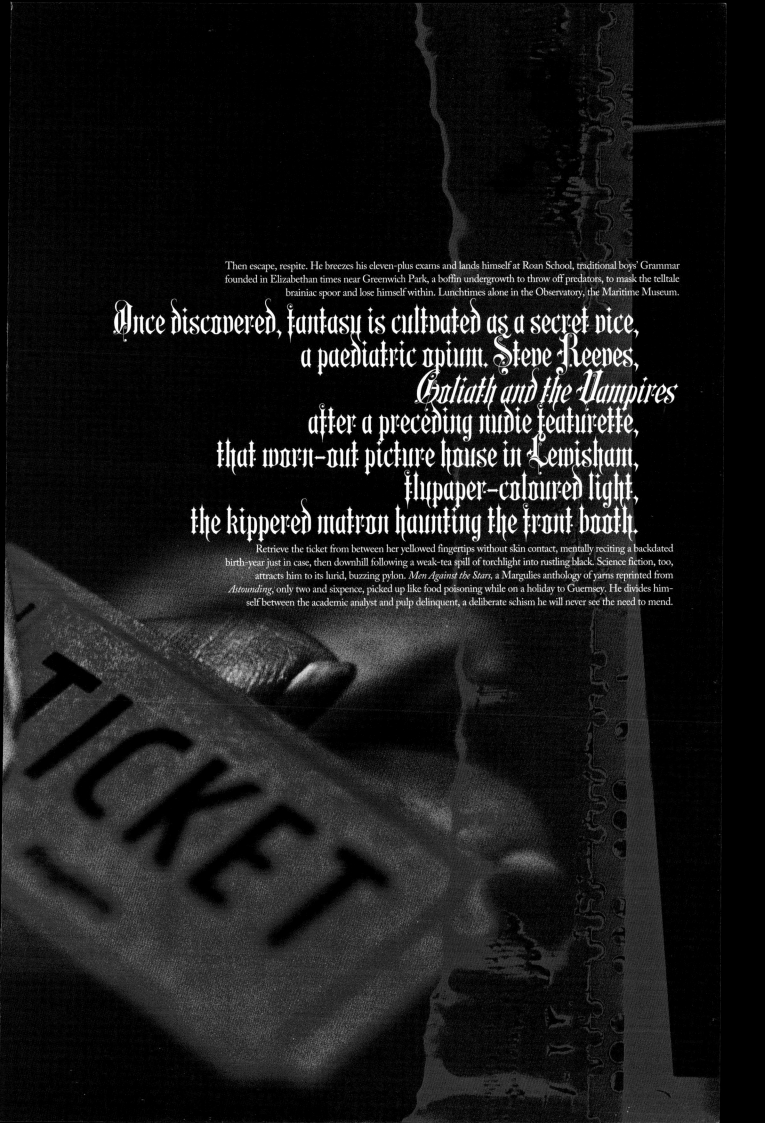

Then escape, respite. He breezes his eleven-plus exams and lands himself at Roan School, traditional boys' Grammar founded in Elizabethan times near Greenwich Park, a boffin undergrowth to throw off predators, to mask the telltale brainiac spoor and lose himself within. Lunchtimes alone in the Observatory, the Maritime Museum.

**Once discovered, fantasy is cultivated as a secret vice,
a paediatric opium. Steve Reeves,
Goliath and the Vampires
after a preceding nudie featurette,
that worn-out picture house in Lewisham,
flypaper-coloured light,
the kippered matron haunting the front booth.**

Retrieve the ticket from between her yellowed fingertips without skin contact, mentally reciting a backdated birth-year just in case, then downhill following a weak-tea spill of torchlight into rustling black. Science fiction, too, attracts him to its lurid, buzzing pylon. *Men Against the Stars,* a Margulies anthology of yarns reprinted from *Astounding,* only two and sixpence, picked up like food poisoning while on a holiday to Guernsey. He divides himself between the academic analyst and pulp delinquent, a deliberate schism he will never see the need to mend.

Failing to realise that his interest IN the scientific has collapsed to a vestigial COVER STORY for his fascination with the FICTIONAL, HE'S carried through his schooldays caught in the remorseless current of the science stream, passing  SIX 'O' LEVELS a year early and then sluiced into a lab job, quality control at Rank-Hovis-McDougall, WHITE-FACED to find that at SIXTEEN he's A *flour grader*. THIS LAST YEAR, SINCE 1964 he's been attending *meetings of the* wilfully progressive LONDON S.F. GROUP at someone's first-floor flat in  Kilburn.

Moorcock is around, there's talk of making an experimental sci-fi movie from Charles Platt and Langdon Jones and every week he rides the night-train home with John Carnell, then editing *New Worlds* and nurturing its fledgling new wave, living just downhill in Plumstead. How has he descended from those crackling, inspiring heights to this, a mere laboratory hunchback, hair a dusty preview of its later self, pay-packet burning less holes in his pockets than the everyday slop of sulphuric acid? He regrets his choice of occupation in a week, stays there for eighteen months, his jeans eventually reduced to smoking lace. Even his first taste of a girlfriend, their eyes meeting over the retorts through a corrosive steam, is not enough to hold his interest. 'Barbara or Louise' falls by the wayside, is supplanted by a new and more enduring passion, a new signal beamed from Uniceptor IV. Early in 1965 he's turned out his first fanzine, *Vega*, printed and distributed by the BSFA, a British amateur science fiction publishing association, thrown himself headlong into the bitchy, blotchy, endlessly enthusiastic circle-jerk of small press magazines, as yet still unaware how closely he is following the fatal H.P. Lovecraft template.

In the Charles Platt-edited **Beyond** *he first reads of the new Yank comic-books, Stan Lee's crowd-pleasing formula of omnipotent losers. Yeah, you may be Nordic God of Thunder, but you've got a gammy leg. You'd trade your spider-senses and ability to run up walls for just ten minutes' tops and fingers. Mythic beings wearing science fiction pants against a mournful and distressed Jack Kirby bowery, paranoid Steve Ditko skyline. How can he resist? Immersing himself in the garish newsprint flood that crosses the Atlantic by erratic spurts, as ballast, he drinks in the warm new smell of raw America. Swiftly acquiring a discerning eye he gravitates towards the somehow more distinguished product issuing from out the stable of Stan Lee's main rival, former Lovecraft literary agent Julius Schwartz. The science fiction here is old school, classical, romantic, perfect men and women on a field of stars,*
described with clean lines, Carmine Infantino's Cadillac-smooth sweep or Gil Kane's Michelangelo anatomies, weightless in sculpted plastic space. He's hooked, and, meeting amiable Brummie

proto-comicfan Phil Clarke at 1965's London-based World S.F. Convention, he decides to put together the UK's first comics fanzine, Ka-Pow #1, dot-screened Adam West onomatopoeia, Roneo spirit-duplicated, purple carbon process, ghostly violet pages with a methylated bombsite tang.
In 1967, fired by new resolve, he says goodbye to

Rank-Hovis-McDougall

goodbye to Louise-or-Barbara, and seeks employment in the Funhouse

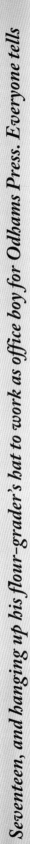

Seventeen, and hanging up his flour-grader's bat to work as office boy for Odhams Press. Everyone tells

him it's a bad idea. He starts there on May 1st to find H.Q. closed for the public holiday when he calls to collect his documents. Free games for May. A jumpy hippy kid, his chestnut hair cautiously inching past his collar, wallflower in the Perfumed Garden, within three months he's the

junior sub-editor of POW!, *Odhams'*

endearingly club-footed stab at duplicating Stan Lee's meteoric rise on this side of the pond. Here he hooks up with the evolving backbone of a future British comic scene, Steve Parkhouse and Mike Higgs, Kevin O'Neill,

a pre-Pre-Raphaelite Barry Windsor-Smith, and has to suffer an alliterative

nickname in the slavishly reprised 'Smilin' Stan' style of Marvel Comics in the U.S.: Sunny Steve Moore, with the planetary attribution so exactly wrong.

Co-organiser of the first comics convention in this country he is founder to an institution he will one day shun in horror, but back then it still seems such a good idea. He's hanging out at Britain's first comics and science fiction bookshop, Dark They Were And Golden Eyed, *a shimmering joss-stick scented fug in Bedfordbury, then in Berwick Street, the offices of* International Times *next door, with Charles Shaar Murray or Mick Farren dropping in to pick up that month's* Silver Surfer *or swap counter-culture quips across the counter with 'Bram' Stokes, the archetypal bead-strung freak proprietor. By '68 he's corresponding with Bob Rickard who within five years will launch the falling-fishes-and-spontaneous-combustion journal* Fortean Times, *he's glorying in the fizz of new ideas, new music, men upon the moon.*

In 1969 I meet him for the first time, marvelling at his lunar lack of mental gravity, the slow and lazy arc of his creative leaps, the silver dustplumes boiling up around his shoes, one small step for a man. By now the exponential creep of his collection, comic books, paperbacks, pulps, fan publishing detritus, has necessitated a forced seizure of the big back bedroom from his elder brother, Chris, who's banished to the boxroom, a comfort-fit coffin just across the tiny landing. Chris is twenty-six by now, offsetting the swung-cat-free claustrophobia of his sleeping quarters with employment in the real world downhill, in his father's footsteps, with a job at the Hercules Powder Company that Frederick Boehm's has by that time become. He'll stay there for another thirteen years then move to bar work for a while before he finds his true vocation as groundskeeper at the Golf Club, tidying the greens where his Dad's rocket-battery was once positioned, crouched absorbed over his work beneath that merciless expanse of sky, pushing his chipped nails down into black soil, into the root-gauze, grounding himself, earthing, while way back in 1969, back home in Chris's former room his younger sibling makes a fair fist at accomplishing its opp...

An ivy carpeting

OF BOOKSHELVES HAS ALREADY CLAIMED TWO WALLS FOR A.E. VAN VOGT, BRADBURY, CHARLES HARNESS, E.C.TUBB, ABE MERRITT, THE UNUSUAL SUSPECTS, COVERS MAD WITH PINK SAND-CITIES AND PRINCESSES, VACUUM CLEAVAGE, CHROME-DIPPED INTERPLANETARY COCK, FOREVER SATURN. UNDER THE ALREADY-SAGGING SINGLE BED HIS FUNNYBOOKS ARE STACKED, THE LYRIC RAY-GUN ROMANCE *ADAM STRANGE*, THE E.C. SCIENCE FANTASIES, WALLY WOOD'S

POLYTHENE-WRAPPED SPACEGIRLS

with trans-solar darkness pooling under their amazing racks,

Al Williamson's bright hypodermic cities soaring out of duotone-fogged fungus-jungle to impale the nebulae.

Insidious four-colour radiation seeps up through the mattress from the piling pages,

incubating benign crystal wireless tumours in the dozing brain and through the fast glass of his new room's wide rear window Lon-

don crawls like animator's putty,

the Post Office Tower,

CANARY WHARF,

THE DOME,

THE WHEEL,

THE GHERKIN,

blossoming and melting in the *Dan Dare* spaceport seethe of the horizon.

He begins to see the city from the ... by-box perspective of a Chinese print

In early 1969 Odhams is folded into Fleetway Publishing,

I.P.C. Magazines being the resultant amalgam and he's one of the few staffers to survive the move.

A close call,

and an impetus towards diversifying,

adding new strings to a bow he hopes to change by stealth into a harp.

Commences writing scripts for comic weeklies, bonsai screenplays.

Wonder Car,

with art supplied by boyhood god Ron Turner,

chief delineator of mid-'fifties cosmic cop *Rick Random,*

prescient name marking the future as a threshold of complexity.

The 1970s are waxing and in his spare time he's working on superior fan publication *Orpheus* with

Barry Smith,

Steve Parkhouse,

Ian Gibson,

an experimental flux of words and images,

attempts to wring some kind of a poetic from decaying orbits,

damaged drives.

going on below. Restless, he lifts from the untroubled, blissful deep-sleep sine-wave dip of the late 'sixties into the uncertain toss and turn to come.

72

in January, on a rare frost-bitten visit to Bob Rickard's place in Birmingham **he**

hits upon the winning mix of cannabis and late-night Hong Kong action flicks

during a showing of **The Sword**, directed by and starring the adaptable Wang Yu. Between mandarin talons yellow magic grips his heart and he goes overboard, goes oriental mental and subscribes to China Reconstructs, pesters his Uncle Don the book importer for impressive hardback tomes on Chinese history to crowd out the Ace Doubles, launches into a lifelong affair with the I Ching, eventual fellowship of the Royal Asiatic Society. Everything changes at the midnight matinee, at the box office with its moving lines. Fate hits the freeze-frame and the coins hang in the winter air.

He wants to make the jump from editorial offices and prospects that he fears may be unsound onto the listing death-trap scaffolding of a freelance existence. Editor of the impeccably hip fanzines *Stardock* and *Gothique* (back cover collage portrait of Frank Zappa made from cops and corner stores and motorcades; an article on the right wing agenda of the superman entitled *Popaganda, or, Why The Blue Beetle Voted For George Wallace*; Ramsey Campbell's penetrating piece on the grotesque in music, San Saens to the Velvet Underground) Stan Nicholls has established his Notting Hill Buddha frame at *Bookends*, a science fiction/comic/head shop out at Chepstow Place.

He's offering a partnership, the opportunity to type up comic scripts during slack periods down in the bookstore's basement, too good to pass up and those freelance assignments keep on coming, bolstering his false sense of security. *Curse of the Faceless Man*, text stories, jungle fables for the Swedish market, Tarzan of Ikea, twenty episodes of sword-and-sorcery romp *Orek the Outlander*. Things look every bit as bright for him as they had for his parents at their new house on the hill in 1938, but this time it's not doodlebugs or German bombers. It's the Met, the Obscene Publications Squad. No warning sirens and no backyard shelter for the R. Crumb cum-shots or the S. Clay Wilson severed pirate-dicks to huddle in until everything's over.

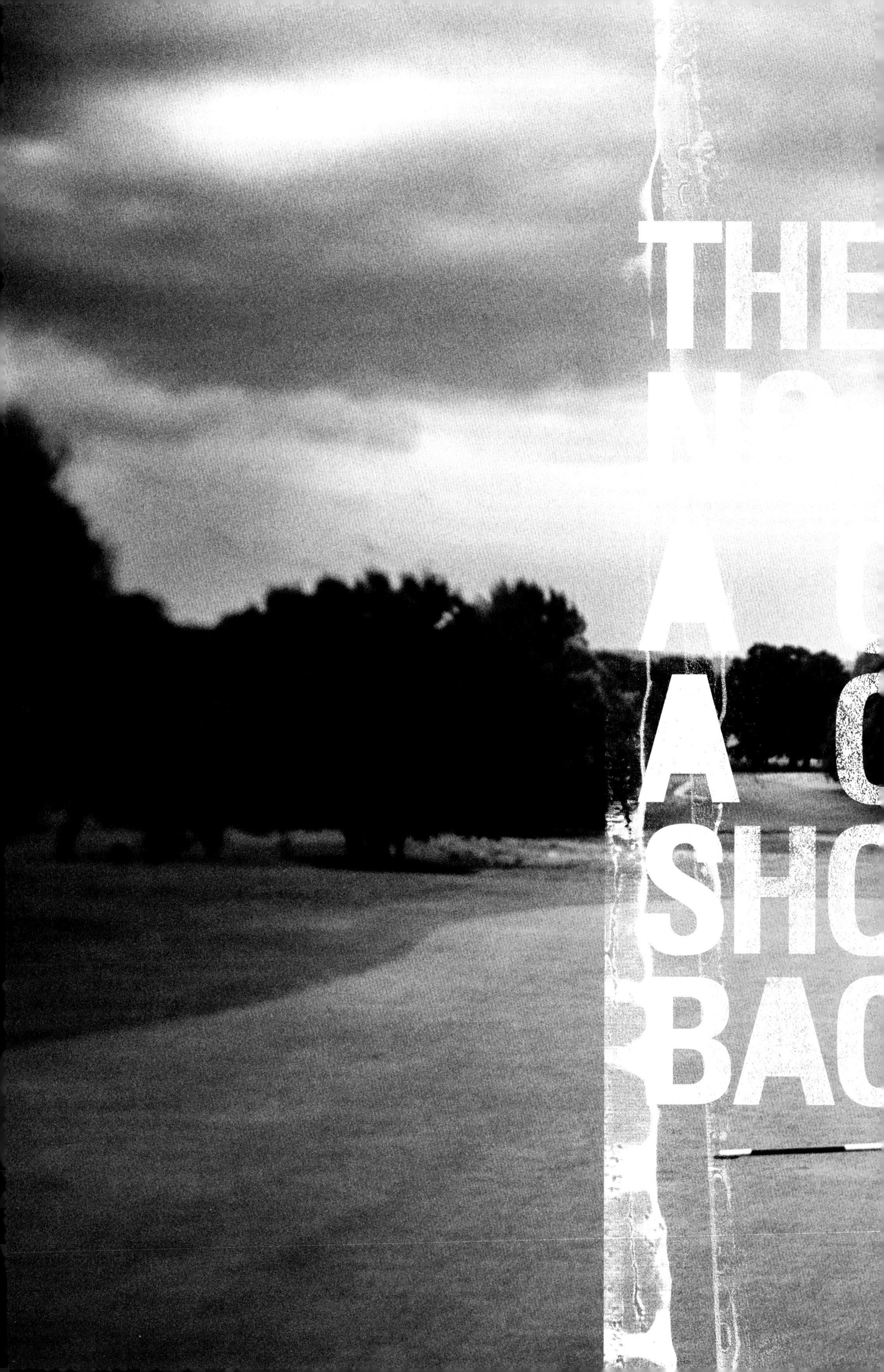
THE

during all this his father dies, a golf-course stroke, just short of turning sixty-five.
The pulmonary guns fire everything they've got into a popping strobe-lit heaven, emptying the chambers.

Busted,

Bookends is shut down, 1973.
He's writing comics to
pay off five grand in business debts,
but it's a largely

love
-less

these days, the glitter long since rubbed from all the stern-eyed starmen, alter-ego icons for more optimistic times. Horror and weirdness, that's his tipple now.

Bob Rickard's launched *Fortean Times*, a small-print black and white blast of excluded news, damned data and Hunt Emerson cartoons from the polymath clutter of his Birmingham bedroom, its shoebox morgue files full of thunderstones and Owlmen, Morgawr, simulacra, Indrid Cold.

Our man elects to pitch in with a study of the mystery beasts at large on Shooters Hill, black panthers, black dogs, Black Shuck, sighted mostly in proximity to the location's many water features, streams and mineral springs and the forgotten River Ket or Quaggy.

He's attempting to relate all this to Taoist principles, the dark and watery Yin, the broken line, while almost unintentionally he begins

TO MAP THE HILL'S IMAGINARY CONTOURS

and astral topographies

for the first time, as if he's only just this moment realised where he is. Meanwhile, the days grind forward measured in worn-out typewriter ribbons.

In '74 he lands a gig at Thorpe & Porter's *House of Hammer*, scripts *The Legend of the Seven Golden Vampires*, captions oozing his still burgeoning obsession with Cathay.

1975, he's writing endless children's annuals, documenting the *Sex Secrets Of Bangkok* for a soft-core relaunch of *Tit Bits*, ducking furtively behind the mystifying pseudonym

of Pedro Henry. When the work is thin, down to the Croxley onionskin, he'll work a day or two for Bram Stokes at the relocated *Dark They Were and Golden Eyed* along the

faintly miserable defile of St. Anne's Court. Conveniently, this is where the Charlie Fort crowd get together once a week to sort their clippings out by category,

BVM or **SHC** or **MIB.**

He has his hand read by a friend of Ion Will, the hero in Ken Campbell's Fortean Caper, and is told that when he's twenty - seven he will meet the woman he is meant for, mantically misled on reaching the appointed age in turn at nineteen a remarkable woman a receptionist a warm-but-personable co-worker at the shop as his intended but she's not she's not she's got a boyfriend, got a monkey, and the railtrack creases in his palm were wrong led only to this abused branch line, this neglected siding

In October, quietly, imperceptibly, the filmy and prismatic bubble of his life explodes, burst by a fingertip, from the outside.

He's bought an exorcism-sword on the first day of the new month, one hundre
and eight Chinese coins, cash coins, the perfect geomantic number, square hole
at their centres, bound together by red thread into the flat shape of a ritual blad
for banishing. A King of Swords, the Hebrew letter that's attributed to his tar
trump being Zain, a sword, his passion for sinology awakened by Wang Yu's *Th
Sword,* and now this. Clearly asking for it, he decides to use his new toy in a firs
time improvised attempt at magic, winging it, asking for guidance and, if it's n
too much trouble, a confirming dream. At 4:00 AM next morning he wakes up
darkness and a male voice whispering a single word into his ear.

At first it's gibberish, another false start like all that matchmaking palmistry, then he re
members where he's come across the word before, a book he'd not especially enjoye
Erotic World of Faerie. It's a poem by John Keats based on a Greek myth, its last fifty line
written at Boxhill, one of the heights visible from Shooters Hill toward the south. It seem
Endymion's a shepherd boy who falls in love with the divine Selene, goddess of the moc
and Moon itself. Reciprocating his affections, she explains that since she is the Queen c
night and dreams, there are no means by which he might be with her always other tha
the death-in-life of an eternal sleep, an offer that he gratefully accepts, and that's it, mor
or less.

Lucian has Endymion on the moon in his *True History*, as pirated by Kar
Friedrich Hieronymus, Baron Von Münchausen, which leads to Robin Wil
liams mugging his way through the role in Terry Gilliam's film ad
aptation.   Frankly,

none of this seems

very promising.

Then the coincidences start, the library angels hurling some required book from the shelves down to the tiled floor at his feet. His life, his human narrative begins to trespass on the draughty borderlines of the Fantastic as defined by Tzvetan Todorov, a literature of hesitation that refuses to decide between a rational or supernatural resolution. Henry James' Turn of the Screw, are spectral entities at work here or has the protagonist gone bonkers? Dreams and signs provoke him to investigate the source material, the unembellished myth, and he accumulates a massive library of classics that will match the still-expanding I Ching and science-fantasy collections, will necessitate surrendering another bedroom wall to academic kudzu. He tracks down the legend's pedigree to Mount Latmos in Turkey, the discovery of caves believed to be the hermit shelters of dream-oracles, luftmensch, their lives spent in the presence of their lunar goddess, on the nod, perhaps dosed up on extracts of her sacred, visionary flower. Was this Endymion, his origin, or maybe an Endymion cult? Shooters Hill, Boxhill, Latmos, something about hills here, hills and caves. There at his research in his anchorite retreat upon the summit he constructs another joint and he considers, gradually identifies, as out beyond his window the decade winds down towards its discontented winter, its plutonium blonde denouement.

Shooters Hill, Box Hill, Latmos something about hills here

FILES & CAVES

This is how it is at the approach of the uncanny, each progression in our comprehension of the concept like a footfall treading softly closer. This is how we act, no awe, no terror, just bland reassurance in our default certainty that this can't possibly be happening. Meanwhile, back on Earth, his native planet, things are going well. Regular work for 2000AD or Marvel Comics' UK satellite, Selene and a smattering of Olympians cavorting with Tom Baker in the slick Dave Gibbons crafted pages that he scripts for Marvel's Dr. Who. Entire Selenic Empires of argent imperatrices fall into decline in the back-story of Laser-Eraser, penned for stylish independent Warrior in 1981.

At this last publication's New Cross comic shop-cum-offices in 1982 he's ruinously smitten once again, picks up another damp and sputtering torch, another big-eyed china doll behind the counter of a mylar-lined emporium. While she's on holiday that summer he completes a first draft of the book-length piece of I Ching scholarship he's working on, Trigrams of Han, a drastic reinterpretation of the oracle which overturns, authoritatively, long decades of accreted dogma on the subject and proposes a more complex and sophisticated model, a mnemonic mapping of the ancient Chinese worldview in its convolute entirety, imagining that this is how one goes about impressing pretty girls.

In 1984

with the demise of *Warrior* he moves with her to a shared house in Westcliff, Essex, the sole change of address he will make during his lifetime. Sticks it for three painful months and then comes home to the familiar bed, familiar view, familiar chair. His mother hasn't touched a thing.

In 1985 he and his brother find one day they cannot wake her and the morning that she didn't make, it's pencil crayon light diffused on the unmoving eiderdown, death like her life demure, transacted without inconveniencing anyone. Mary, whom he took after. Every other night she still calls from the kitchen in his dreams.

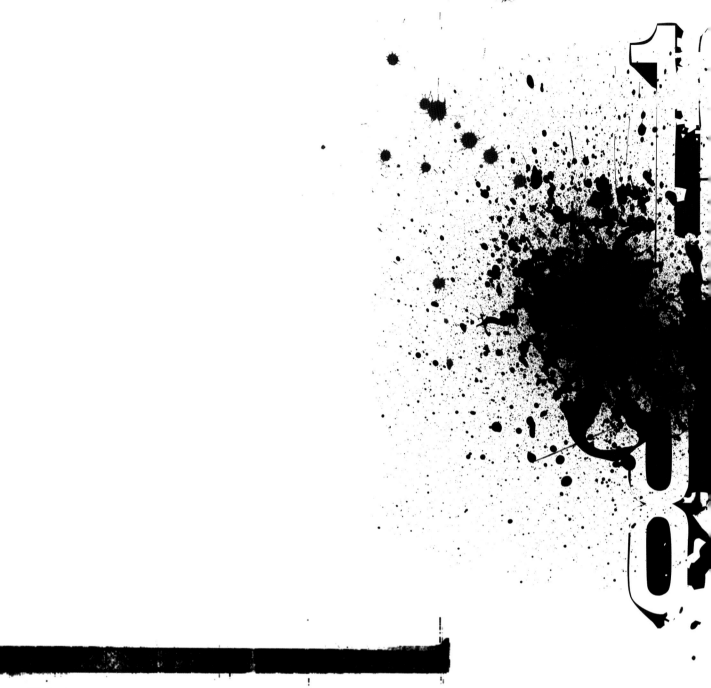

The 'eighties burn down, guttering, with so much gone and melted. Westcliff woman married with a kid, they still think of each other as good friends but, well, you know. His mum's gone too, these stabilising female gravities, these planets breaking from his system, spinning off into the stars.

The only woman who re-
tains her influence upon
him lives in Downing Street,
is running down herself with
supervillain tic in one eye,
one hard now a pincer,
WILL BE GONE
WITHIN A YEAR.

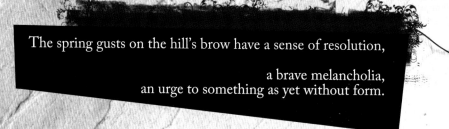

The spring gusts on the hill's brow have a sense of resolution,

a brave melancholia,
an urge to something as yet without form.

For reasons that he only poorly understands he has the sudden yen to dust off undeveloped drawing skills left on a high shelf since those early fanzine days, just for the exercise. Best start with something small. Small and erotic, to ensure that the enthusiasm needed to complete the project is maintained, Bog-Venus logic. Knows himself too well.

He starts to paint the body of the goddess, of the female that he first encountered in '76, the foretold age of twenty-seven, couchant on a ground of turquoise night, naked except for her stephane, her crown, the spill of auburn splashing down upon her breasts, her shoulders. She sits unselfconsciously, her legs apart, déjeuner sur l'herbe. He tries to make her face that of his recently lost love but here the licked-sharp brush refuses, cleaving to its own agendas. Diamond highlights animate the eyes, the gaze engaged, amused and up for trouble. For a while her smile eludes him, long nights' precious labour on her lips, the dawning knowledge that this graven image, this commandment-breaker, is the seal of an insoluble commitment. After something like a week she's finished, the addictive toil curtailed, contained within the narrow wooden limits of a prop-up frame to sit beside the armchair he makes notes in, on the desk he types at, by his bed. You saw me standing alone, without a dream in my heart, without a love of my own. The shape made by her limp white limbs becomes a tender rune, an ampersand belonging to an alphabet of greater passion, stronger meaning, drinking in the energy of his attention, of his writing, of his work, his sex, his sleep until the framed glass hums with it, lenses the trapped vibrations back into the room's air-pocket ambience, a high pitched alpha drone on its periphery. Emotionally compressed the bubble habitat heats up, exhibits sonoluminescence, starts to shine.

Over the next few years the sense of contact ebbs and flows, never recedes entirely while he's busy with the US colour version of Laser-Eraser, earning, yearning, finishing Trigrams of Han and finding it a publisher on money that his mum has left, or grafting as a contract writer/editor for the going concern that Fortean Times, increasingly, has started to become. Viz magnate John Brown is the magazine's new publisher, its circulation rising as its genuinely interesting hardcore content dips, its articles on lexical linkages or its psychometric scrying of American arcana shunted out in favour of X-Files-related cover features, rubber Roswell autopsies. A bigfoot stumble, coughing in the dust of a bandwagon as it rumbles off to disappear forever into Area 51. Meanwhile the postcard-sized framed portrait has become the portal where he stands and stares, replacing the grand panorama of the outer world beyond his bedroom window with its moonless view. She's there behind the glass, a different universe just millimetres from his fingertips, with everything she represents.

Divine light.

THE ROMANCE

SORCERY

Aleister Crowley calls it a disease of language.
Spot it from a mile off, the enflamed vocabulary, the light-headed syntax.
Luckily, most of the population have been immunised by

C.S. LEWIS, TOLKIEN, J.K. ROWLING, BUFFY,

by exposure to the virus in the form of a dead culture,
something that will force no-nonsense antibodies to kick in without the danger of full-blown enchantment.
Texts that act as disinfectant, language pasteurised for ordinary consumption,
all the ontological blue mould scraped off, the strange loops of self reference, the pathogens,
words so far past their best-before date that they're crawling, they're alive.

Virulent

is t

Warily investigating, he affiliates himself in 1992 to a magical order, The Illuminates of Thanateros, temple a New Cross recording studio. Chaos magic, though the name seems harsh. Bit of a mess at worst, more teen goth's bedroom than inchoate pre-creational abyss. He chants along with all the others for a while, recalls his lip-synched prayers at school assembly, then has the temerity to enquire of an order head if there's a reason why the ceremonial robes have to be black, is told in lieu of answer that it shows colossal ignorance to even ask. God, what if everybody questioned the most basic principles of ritual like that? It'd be chaos.

Clearly not for him, warmed-over Austin Osman Spare without requirement to tread too close to the edge of the apocalyptic Brixton artist/shaman's risky line. He holds out for a month or two then jacks it in, though not without a certain fidgety dissatisfaction, an impatience with the numinous. You get all dressed up and she doesn't show. You turn up at the juju showroom to take magic for a test drive and can't get it off the lot, while all the senior salesmen stand around and suck their teeth. Maybe it hasn't got an engine, maybe that whole internal combustion thing was only crazy talk, and yet the promise in her eyes, behind the glass, beside the bed.

There must be more to wizardry than this, this Gandalf-with-his-knob-pierced stuff.

Where's the romantic rush,

the Blake ache? Where's

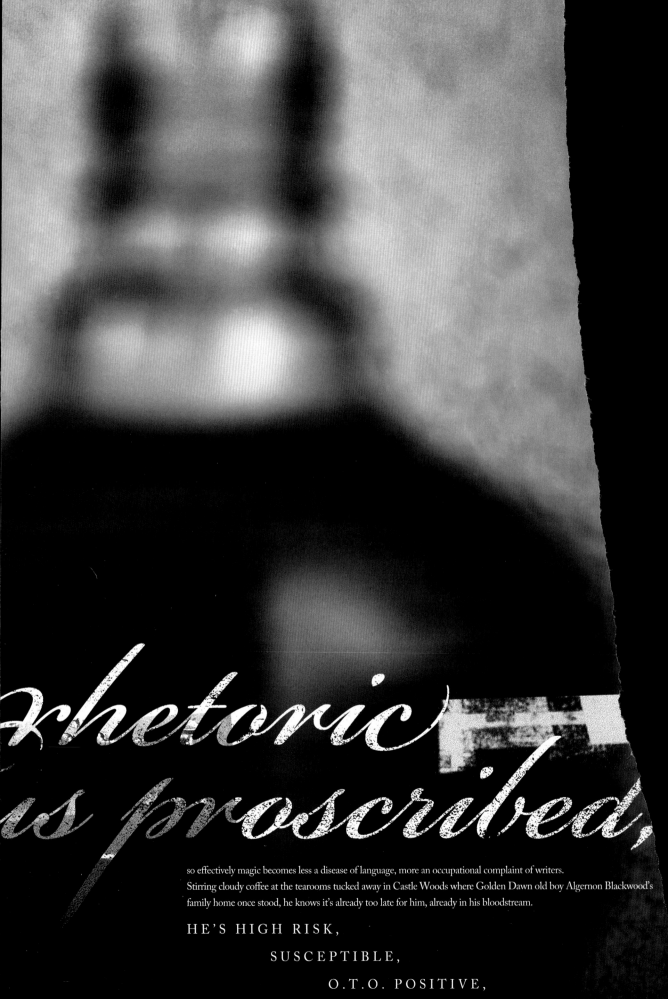

rhetoric) as proscribed,

so effectively magic becomes less a disease of language, more an occupational complaint of writers.

Stirring cloudy coffee at the tearooms tucked away in Castle Woods where Golden Dawn old boy Algernon Blackwood's family home once stood, he knows it's already too late for him, already in his bloodstream.

HE'S HIGH RISK,

SUSCEPTIBLE,

O.T.O. POSITIVE,

the *I Ching* work and covert goddess-worship markers of occult predisposition

ghosts

Visiting him, January 7th,
1994,
the cab ride up from
Lewisham
through
Blackheath

WITH ITS

The Bronze Age rabble who weren't on the list when they were handing out the hilltop burial mounds. Montague Druitt, cricketer and fit-up Ripper suspect with his astral doppelganger David Lindsay, author of *A Voyage to Arcturus*, translucent fantasy that opens at a London séance then progresses into fiery allegorical terrain that characters must sprout new sensory organs even to perceive. The taxi shifts down, struggling up the hill towards its brink, and there is the familiar illusion that this raised, uncomfortably close horizon may have only sheer drop on the other side. Set down beside the road with rubies shoaling in the rush-hour dark, across from the Memorial Hospital, then those few paces down an almost-hidden

footpath and into the sheltering close,

through

its paper-lantern light warm

the Art?

t this point the narrator, up to now concealed behind the safety curtain, trying to keep out of it, must advertise his presence with a cough without allowing this to turn to a hn Silence story, to a yarn where the intrepid house-on-haunted-hill investigator is reluctantly, predictably drawn in and made a witness to the awful outcome, to the anishing, the giant hand from beyond. I've been along with him for most of the above, entranced and fascinated, following his lead, convinced that the smart money was on is unlikely scarecrow. **All About Eve**, him as Bette Davis. Follow him into the drug-fug of the 'sixties underground and through the Fortean ruminations of the 'seventies; ato the comic-writing thing, his red corrections vivid and instructive lacerations on those first trial scripts, twenty-five years back. In the early 'nineties with a three-lane ile-up of a marriage still receding in the rear-view mirror, following him into magic seems a good idea, a way to steer the vehicle of writing off the speedway of career to fluorescent wasteland. His forays in organised contemporary magical society, all his New Cross necromantic nights, are watched with interest. Let's see if this sends him ad or kills him before making any personal investment. Sharing his frustration and his disappointment when it fizzles out without result, late night conversations as to what genuinely modern magic worldview might entail, more literary and progressive, texts to represent the body of the god that may in some way then be treated or manipulated, et/Osiris, Burroughs/Gysin, two cut-up techniques somehow reduced to one, the psilocybin dialogues blithely wandering through riff, hypothesis and rant towards hidden precipice.

rnng

of

pulled - to

teatime

curtains.

Welcomed in, cursory head-poke round the door into the soccer-highlight grumble of the living room to say hello to Chris, past fifty now and looking forward to early retirement from groundskeeping thanks to a pool syndicate win some years earlier, a notable example of the elder sibling's striking-if-ambiguous relationship with probability and football, since he'll later lose one eye to flesh-eating infection in a minor wound sustained during his Sunday morning kick-about. A game of two halves, clearly. After packing in the job he'll fill his time, he'll fill his half-share of the house

with Cacti succulents,

that most extra-terrestrial of plants, speaking of an emotional reserve, survival in a hostile, dry environment, the water and the sweetness held inside. He and his brother with their amiably parallel existences will see the hilltop house become a border skirmish-zone, part of some age-old territorial war between the science fiction paperbacks and the asclepiads. Exchanging genuine pleasantries with Chris, the next stop is his brother's room, the humming gem-field of its northern vista and signature two-note tinkle from the old and delicate tin wind chimes just inside the door.

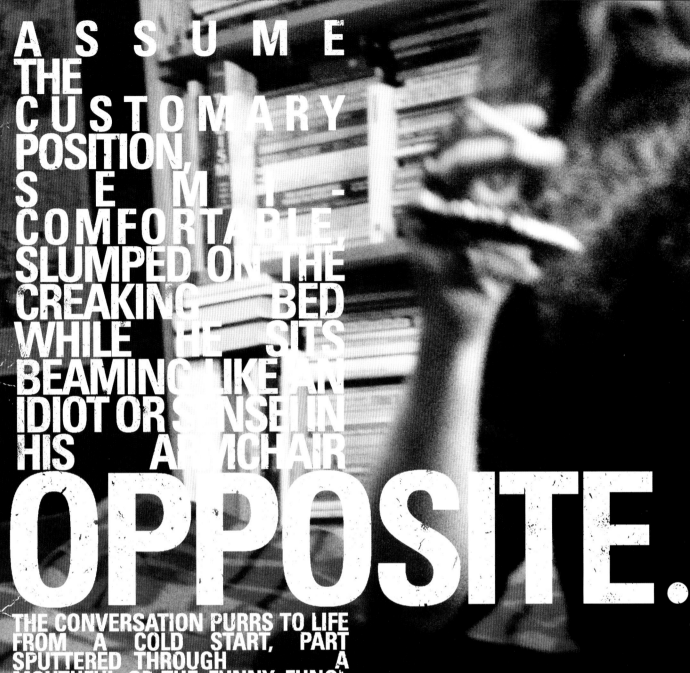

ASSUME THE CUSTOMARY POSITION, SEMI-COMFORTABLE, SLUMPED ON THE CREAKING BED WHILE HE SITS BEAMING LIKE AN IDIOT OR SENSEI IN HIS ARMCHAIR OPPOSITE.

THE CONVERSATION PURRS TO LIFE FROM A COLD START, PART SPUTTERED THROUGH A MOUTHFUL OF THE FUNNY FUNGI, MILDEWED SPIDER-ROE, ROUTINE AND PURELY RECREATIONAL, A SEMI-REGULAR AND CASUAL FEATURE OF THE PREVIOUS FIFTEEN YEARS.

The talk drifts easily to magic in the slow three-quarter hour approach to lift-off, something complicated, foggy, about gods as texts, linguistic entities, so if you inter-cut two texts together, say a god and goddess, then what kind of fusion might result, but wait a minute, wait a minute, that's not what he's saying, pay attention, it's this other stuff with one text seen as corpus of the goddess and the other one a purely hermaphrodite, as alloy, tempered gold and silver, chemic wedding, this is crucial, this is so important although actually that isn't quite what he's attempting to convey, we're at cross-purposes, it's more the notion of a statement of intent, a page of writing, then you take another page, an invocation to the god or goddess and you cut them up and shuffle them together so that purpose and divinity are one, so, let's see, that would mean that in the union of two passages composed to represent the male and female deities there would be a new sexual alchemy, is that right, and the struggle to express this, this is all so difficult and Jesus man, we've just, we've just been through this, through this exact, this exact same conversation

THREE THREE THREE TIMES

THREE TIMES

and something stoops,
leans in from outside,
gathering identity with its approach,
It pushes its unfathomable face down into our aquarium,
displacing world,
spilling reality on Heaven's front-room floor.

We're flopping breathless on the holy carpeting. This isn't meant to happen. We aren't doing anything, we're only talking and we stumble on an idea that turns out to be connected to another, then another, and the discourse makes its labouring progress upward from one concept to the next, completely unaware of climbing something's tail until it flicks, an active spirochete attending this disease of language. Dream-spine, knobbly with conceptual vertebrae but smooth as viscous liquid in its movement, living chain of muscular and dangerous notion, looping and recursive thought-meat winding, coiling back and forth upon itself, a current dragging helpless consciousness along its length in rippling peristalsis. Churning in this burning gold confusion, the awareness of having been swallowed by a snake of some kind is belated, useless, and we're riding the King's Highway, slamming primary-colour neon bumpers in the sephirothic pinball, shrieking like a roller coaster in the ricochet from zone to zone. Zone where both parties realise things could happen here, things that could shatter friendship irretrievably, and dare not speak the thought out loud. Zone where both parties realize simultaneously that they have been alone in this hallucination, none of this has really happened, that they have gone mad and all this time their colleague has been minding them, distressed, concerned, may have already called the ambulance,

LOOK,

LOOK,

at all that worry in his

EYES.

ZONE LIKE A ROOM OF DAZZLING WHITE, *full of dead magi*

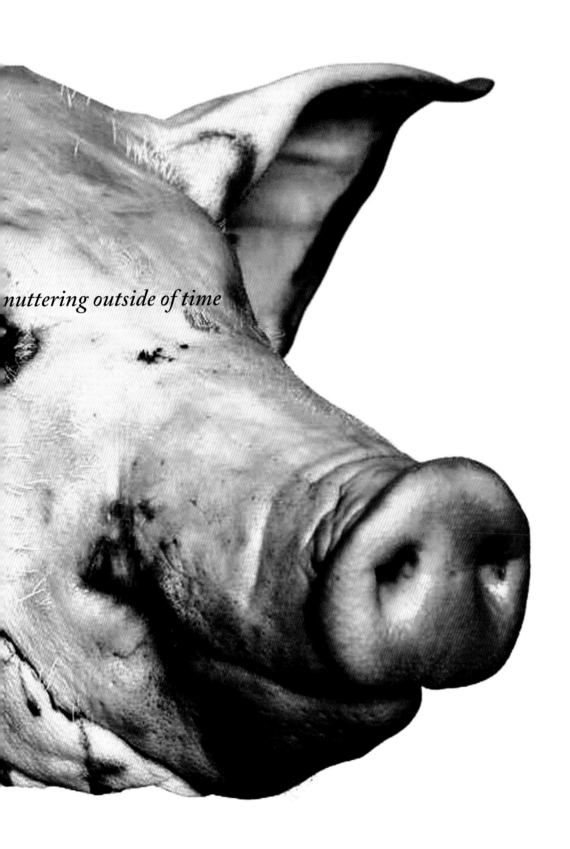

nuttering outside of time

when you die

Increasingly, this includes his relationship with the tarot-scale image of the goddess resting on the shelf beside his bed. Where previously the conceit of a fond, romantic folly has provided insulation from the stark insanity of what he's been half-entertaining, now the gloves are off. The poetry has jumped the fence and threatens rampage in his proudly-maintained china shop of rationality. Todorov's definition of Fantastic literature as hesitation, as deferment of one's choice between a psychological or an unearthly explanation, has become his tightrope, and successful subsequent experiments with sorcery don't make things any better. She gets more real every night, is in his dreams, will sometimes break beyond the confines of the sexualised imaginary friend, of her allotted moon-nymph role, and show another face. He dreams he's in his room, almost aware that he is dreaming, almost lucid, kneeling by his bed to fumble underneath it for some misplaced Planet Stories *pulp and*

suddenly she's standing there behind him and he doesn't dare look round. Her voice, from over his left shoulder as he kneels, is not that of the young girl in his painting. This is someone older talking, someone graver with a ring of sad authority. *There are bad times ahead, and yet because you love me, so shall I protect you.*

When you die, you will become a lily.'

He looks rough on visits to Northampton during 1995,

passes out once or twice in public, and the magical experiments are steadily accumulating their own spooky aura. Lose each other for a moment in the busy main street's weekend shove, look round to find the other party gone, both struck by the same thought, what if we never saw the other man again? Magic is all about expanding the parameters of what is possible, and thin air suddenly seems like a possibility. That year he starts as editor of erudite and handsome Fortean Studies, a new journal launched by Fortean Times to make a home for all the fascinating academic stuff displaced by glowering spreads of Gillian Anderson, David Duchovny. Gleefully, he puts together dense anthologies of mysteries and marvels, wonders crowded to the margins by an influx of grey aliens and anal probes. The phantom Russian troops, 'snow on their boots', reported marching from the north of England during World War II to make a sneak attack on Germany. A self-penned contribution on the possible historic authenticity or otherwise of strange Chinese automata, the wooden oxen said to have been engineered by Chinese Merlin-figure Chu-ko Liang in 230 AD or thereabouts. Another piece of his on enigmatic and reputedly lunar secretions, some form of celestial cuckoo-spit known to antiquity as 'moon-foam'. This is much more like it. This is something he can get his teeth into, research and facts and dates and accurate investigation, publishing perfectionism. This is heavy, a huge intellectual anchor to prevent him drifting upwards, off into the mist, into the moonlight. Just in case, he adds some extra ballast: an exhaustive indexing by topic of Fortean Times for 1993 which will eventually lead to indexing the entire quarter-century of the magazine's duration, then The Oracle, a scholarly small press journal of I Ching studies that he edits, then a massive bibliography of I Ching reference, from Crowley to John Cage that he embarks on in collaboration, something for those idle moments.

Worried by his spazz-attacks and b
1996 is told he has high blood pre
cardiac catastrophe waiting to happe
help

puts he checks with a doctor and in
e, though not that he's a high-risk
nich presumably they figure wouldn't

He cuts down on the smoking and goes for a recommended walk each day around the hilltop, lanes and avenues he's not set foot in since his childhood. It's a revelation, the variety of architectural styles, the sudden incongruities in rows otherwise uniform that mark a buzz bomb hit. Magnificently monstrous water tower, a red brick fortress hulking there just past the Bull, and blue cut-paper torrents of hydrangea overflowing the low garden walls to spill into the streets. The post-box with a primitive horned stick-man sprayed in black upon its violent red. He taps into his family history, the blood-roots sunk into the bloodhill, reconnects with his environment and becomes reacquainted with its quanta, with its charge and spin, its strangeness and its charm.

Partway through 1998 while he's engaged, contentedly, in juggling his various and complex intellectual responsibilities, The Oracle, Fortean Studies, I Ching bibliography and the by-now deranging Fortean Times index, his neglected love life coughs once, sits up naked on the slab and says 'Where am I?' just when everyone has given up on it. An E-affair, a dotcom romcom, a subscriber to The Oracle that he's been corresponding with who's fallen for him, wants to meet him. For God's sake, he's nearly fifty and he really doesn't need this; needs this desperately. She's an I Ching diviner teaching Taoist meditation and the yogic discipline Qi Gong. She lives in South America and if he'd care to he can pop out for a visit, stay there at her Dad's coffee plantation for a while, her place in Rio or the beach house in Bahia. He's convinced that he's been given pages from somebody else's script, casting department oversight, but still decides to play along, see how far he can get with normal human life

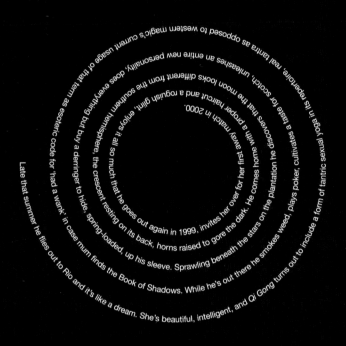

Late that summer he flies out to Rio and it's like a dream. She's beautiful, intelligent, and Qi Gong turns out to include a form of tantric sexual yoga in its repertoire, real tantra as opposed to western magic's current usage of that term as esoteric code for 'had a wank' in case mum finds the Book of Shadows. While he's out there he smokes weed, plays poker, cultivates a taste for scotch, unleashes an entire new personality, does everything but buy a derringer to hide, spring-loaded, up his sleeve. Sprawling beneath the stars on the plantation he discovers that the moon looks different from the southern hemisphere, the crescent resting on its back, horns raised to gore the dark. He comes home with a proper haircut and a roguish glint, enjoys it all so much that he goes out again in 1999, invites her over for her first away match in 2000.

ENGLAND

understandably,

is something of a shock to the Brazilian system.

Life's a beach and then you hit South London, where the heat-waves bring her out in goosebumps. Meets and likes his one-eyed brother Chris, whom thanks to errors in translation she'd assumed to be an evil cyclops keeping Steve a prisoner in his lonely garret room, forced to hang underneath the belly of a ram if he should want to nip out to the shops, but even her relief does not endear the landscape to her. The astounding northern prospect of the city from his bedroom window is just city, lacking coast or mountains can't be called a view. The overcast skies, sunsets on a black and white TV when she's been used to colour.

When she goes back home they part

as lovers but at Heathrow there's a

shift in indoor light, perhaps a

misfire in the

a premonition.

Her black hair and coffee skin are melted,

stirred into the milky pallor

swirling there in the

DEPARTURE LOUNGE.

Returning to his work he feels a certain apprehension in the air, a V-bomb hush that makes him restless, reckless. All this editorial responsibility will drive him bugfuck if he doesn't make a break,

and so he quits *Fortean Studies* after issue six, concludes the indexing and bibliography, then extricates himself with honour from commitments to his Oracle subscribers and throws in the towel. He's got a couple of new projects on the go that will drain off the excess energy, a thorough excavation of the mythological Selene that might rescue the original text-body of the goddess from beneath a palimpsest of re-sprays, Robert Graves and Women's Mysteries, restore her to her former glory. This is something that's been brewing since '76 but now he's getting down to business, loosely mapping out the necessary chapters and then there's this other thing, this idea out of nowhere, for a novel. Something based upon the elements that have defined his life thus far, the hilltop solitude, the moon, the quarter-century back-catalogue of dreams.

He tinkers with the notion in the evenings, wants to craft an unadulterated night-work. Now that he's not smoking any more he finds he likes a glass of scotch or three to help his mind uncoil into the still-coagulating narrative. Currently having something of a crush on the Elizabethans he's not listening to anything except gavottes, pavanes, speed garage harpsichord extravaganzas that put him in mind of his most cherished 'sixties vinyl, Hendrix or the Yardbirds, a Jeff Beck deluge of notes. The sixteenth century aural filigree infects his prose, informs his thinking with a tendency to the elaborate, an urge to decorate. By day he's come full circle, writing comic scripts for the increasingly nostalgic-sounding *2000AD,* the weekly publication traipsing nervously into its namesake year, the single dazed survivor of a homegrown comics industry that's suffered an extinction event, a migration of the native talent to America after the British comics boom exemplified by *Warrior.* The thriving field he'd given up flour grading for all of those years ago is nearly dead, almost entirely vanished, the attendant fanzine scene turned into purple dust, all blown away and somehow, when you think about it, this is probably his fault. In normal working hours he writes the space-Yakuza yarn *Red Fang* and the Clark Ashton Smith-like *Tales of Telguuth* as atonement,

but when darkness falls he pours himself a shot, cranks up Now That's What I Call Harpsichords *full volume and applies himself to his new secret labour, the new edifice he's building out of dark and drink and dreams, out of Elizabethan reggae and the hilltop's gutter-dust.*

He's even found a word, a name that's rattling around inside his head, a working title.

'SOMNIUM'. Perhaps a city, lost.
Perhaps an element not yet unearthed,
not yet discovered.

Late 2000, early 2001,

he gets the email from Brazil that he's been half-expecting, breaking off the romance. They're in different hemispheres, they're under different moons. They need less space. He's upset, but the cracked chime in the gut is somehow muffled, or at least held in abeyance. What it is, he's picking up a lot of interference on the Venus waveband, garbled bursts of an emotive Morse he can't unscramble. Intermittently across the years he's been in casual, amiable contact with the yummy mummy that his botched Westcliff elopement has become, is matey with her husband and her son, visits her maybe once a year, all that old heartache done with and behind him, pretty much. But now, with perfect or perfectly dreadful timing her married life detonates and she's pinned underneath the rubble of divorce, no feelings in her numb extremities, calling out weakly, asking if there's anybody there. She badly needs some reassurance, as you do, to feel desirable, attractive and, okay, so if one night she hits the wine too hard and sends out some ambiguous signals then that's understandable. That's understandable to anyone who's been there, anyone but him. He gets the diagnosis wrong, completes the crossword clue that's in her late night phone calls far too hastily though he has no more than the first two letters, guesses 'loving' when in fact the answer's

he's dis- orient- ed

and all this sentimental sediment is filtered through the whiskey into Somnium, the plot of which has by now crystallised into a mirror, is about a lovelorn writer who appears to be losing his mind on top of Shooters Hill. 'Appears to be', so you can see that he's still clinging onto Tzvetan Todorov's Fantastic get-out clause, dangling from one end of the lifeline that was formerly his tightrope. This could yet resolve itself into a supernatural narrative rather than one of psychological collapse, Turn of the Screw. There's still that hesitation to hang onto, although frankly the sheer misery distilled into the prose makes it progressively more slippery, harder for anybody to maintain that vital grip, especially him. His main protagonist's a nineteenth century author who's retreated from a doomed infatuation to seclusion in his rooms at the Bull Inn there on the hilltop. As a solace, a distraction from self-pity, he starts work upon a novel that's entitled Somnium, a wild romantic fantasy that's set on Shooters Hill during Elizabethan times. Already in this outline, in this book-within-a-book, the surface eddies that could deepen to a whirlpool are apparent but he presses on regardless. An Elizabethan knight, the hero of this second Somnium, rides to the hill upon a moonlit night and finds a hinge between two worlds, a different hilltop with a luminous marmoreal palace, giant architecture a stylistic hybrid between Mucha and Vitruvius, where dwells the incarnated lunar goddess Diana Regina. The affair develops as a convex version of Beardsley's erotic fantasy Under the Hill, and meanwhile in his room at the Bull Inn the bereft nineteenth century author of all this is having dreams, with statuary and pillars from his novel found in cellars underneath the hostelry, begins to lose sight of a line between his writing and real

Despite the dry-ice gothic cold-front gathering around his life and fiction, it becomes quite clear that, speaking psychologically, the re twenty-first century author of Somnium is setting up a flawless piece of slapstick for himself, becoming Michael Crawford at some gruesome halfway poi between Frank Spencer and the Phantom of the Opera. He's got the roller skates, the plank, the tub of paste, the shopping cart. He's got the steep hill. All needs is one good circumstantial shove, something the audience could see coming from a mile away, and a hilarious mix-up will most certainly ensue with h careening off into the laugh-track.

It's around this point.

that he receives a message from his Westcliff wisp of smoke, never exactly an old flame, inviting him as a much-valued chum to share her happiness at finding a new boyfriend, and it all comes down on him at once. The loss of his Brazilian woman, a deferred ache, and now this, the long shot everything was riding on, gone down at the first fence. He's drinking, riding on the redeye, and in *Somnium* his anguished nineteenth century narrator's drinking too. He wants to die. He's dreaming blocks of excavated architecture from his novel just like his increasingly deranged protagonist, exquisite marble shards of an Elizabethan buried moon-town poking up from cellar floors, out of the hilltop dirt.

His brother Chris is by now chairman of a local cactus-fanciers cabal,

is seed-bank secretary to the International Asclepiad Society, is editor and publisher of the society's gazette, the same Gemini energy and King of Swords perfectionism as his younger sibling. Chris announces that he's travelling to South Africa during September,

perfect opportunity to find exotic specimens, weird flowers that stink like dogshit to attract the pollinating blowflies of a country without butterflies or bees. Chris plans to be away for a whole month, the first time his kid brother will have been alone there in the house that long, and right when ideologically he's at his most precarious extreme, could maybe use someone around the house to talk to who's not in his manuscript, not in his head. He goes the whole hog, plans to use the enforced solitude as background for a magical retreat, a scaled-down Abramelin ritual, withdrawal from the world into a strange hermetic space that in all likelyhood turns out to be an

His journal for September is a soberly recounted twilight travelogue, a disaffected radio-telescope view of our planet from some distant satellite. He rigorously records his nightly dreams and daily disciplines, the periods of meditation and the visualisation exercises, yogic practices he learned in South America but has since customized to suit Selene-worship. Where he'd once sat with a human partner straddling his lap, their breathing circling the energy up through his chakras, down through hers, he tries the same thing now while he imagines his moon-deity astride him and it feels the same, the same sense of a shared force circulating and he knows it's mad, he knows it's tragic,

THIS IMAGINARY LOVE, THIS COMPENSATORY DELUSION. but h

gathering substance

feels her
feels her
striving to break through.

'S READING ALEXANDRA DAVID-NEEL, THE WRITINGS ON TIBET, PAYING PARTICULAR ATTENTION TO HER PLAINLY-TOLD FIRST-
AND ACCOUNT OF MANUFACTURING A *TULPA*, A PROJECTED THOUGHT FORM PICTURED WITH SUCH VIVID AND SUSTAINED FEROC-
Y THAT OTHER PEOPLE CAN PERCEIVE IT TOO. CAN TOUCH IT. IF HE VENTURES OUT TO BUY PROVISIONS SHE ACCOMPANIES HIM,
R IMAGINED FORM BECOMING GRADUALLY MORE STABLE, STILL THERE IF HE LOOKS AWAY AND BACK AGAIN, THE NAKED LUNAR
DDESS ON HIS ARM BETWEEN THE PARKED CARS AND THE PRIVET HEDGE, DELVAUX BY DAYLIGHT. IT'S A FAMOUS ABRAMELIN
E EFFECT, LIKE CROWLEY UP AT BOLESKINE WITH SPIRITS THRONGING ON THE TERRACES. THEY CHAT WHILE STROLLING, TRADE
E TRIVIA OF THE CROSSROADS AND HE HEARS HER VOICE, HER CHILDISH WONDERMENT AT THE MUNICIPAL AND THE MUNDANE
FORE THEY HEAD BACK FOR THEIR *QI GONG* PRACTICE IN THE EMPTY OLD HOUSE.

HOME ALONE?

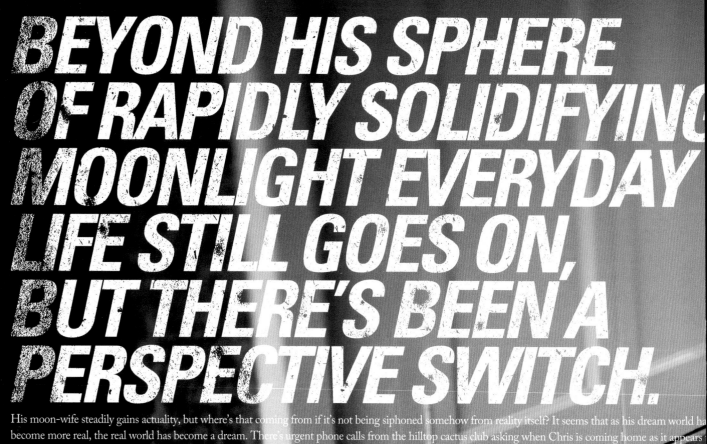

BEYOND HIS SPHERE OF RAPIDLY SOLIDIFYING MOONLIGHT EVERYDAY LIFE STILL GOES ON, BUT THERE'S BEEN A PERSPECTIVE SWITCH.

His moon-wife steadily gains actuality, but where's that coming from if it's not being siphoned somehow from reality itself? It seems that as his dream world ha[s] become more real, the real world has become a dream. There's urgent phone calls from the hilltop cactus club asking when Chris is coming home as it appears [the] treasurer has murdered his own mother and then tried to kill himself, Agatha Christie fiction, spatter on antimacassar and the spiny desert flora potted on a windowsill, green-grey, so difficult to dust.

ON THE ELEVENTH

OF THE MONTH

he scrupulously makes his journal entry for that evening, noting length of time that meditations were sustained throughout the day with details of results, remarking casually in passing that apparently some hijacked planes have been flown into buildings in New York. His only comment is the observation that even apparently rock-solid mass consensual reality can flip into a new, unprecedented state as easily as can the shifting flow of situations in a dream or nightmare, just like that. He finishes the entry, stands and crosses to the window, blinking at the urban nebula suspended floating on the dark outside as he removes his spectacles and cleans them, wipes away the city that's reflected in each lens. Replacing them, he stands and listens to the silent bedroom for a moment, then he nods and chuckles in reply.

Downstairs the woman next door's hall clock sounds the quarter hour.

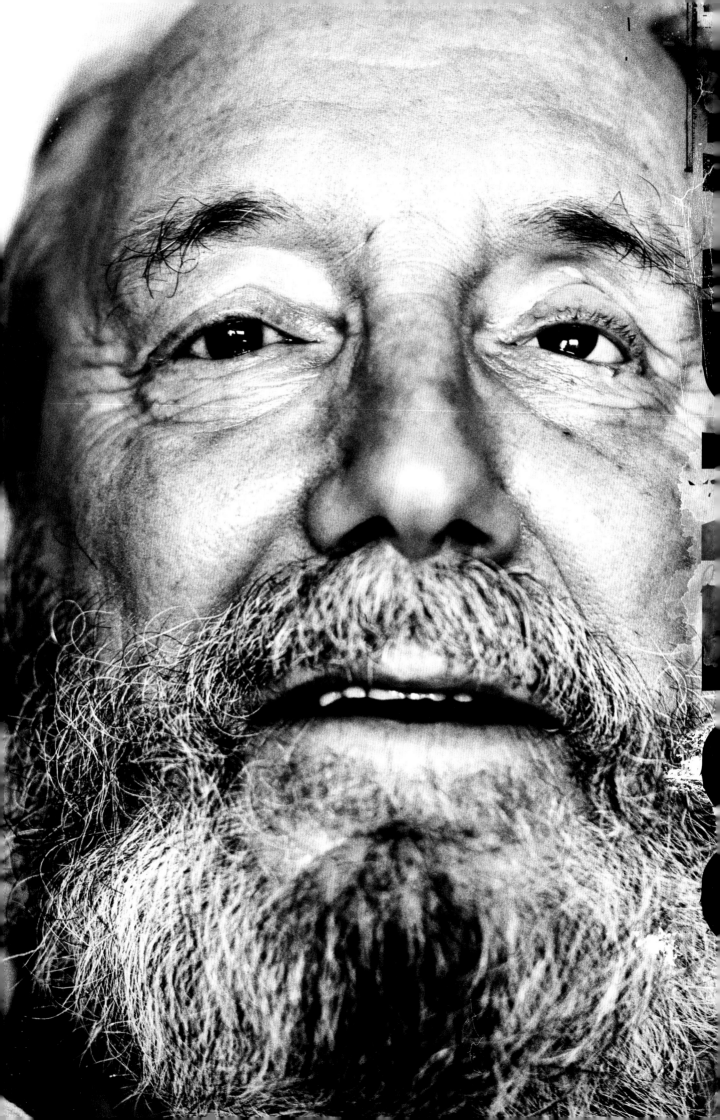

September ENDS,

and with it the retreat. His brother returns with a suitcase full of rare African monsters and becomes the cactus club's new treasurer, takes over from the previous incumbent, now incarcerated. Life at Jim and Mary's 1930s dream-home soon gets back to normal, but with a Greek goddess lodging there in the back bedroom. He cuts down the drinking drastically and keeps up the Selenic ritual practices in one form or another, even now his hermitry is ended. His relationship with her becomes domestic, comfortable, as his relationship with his imagination similarly sees improvements, unsurprisingly when that's the faculty in him she represents. He's cut back on the madrigals and the Elizabethan authors to immerse himself within an absinthe-haze of decadents, Theophile Gautier and Ernest Dowson and Richard Le Gallienne with that inspiring bifurcated afro 'do. He's crafting some of his best work, revising *Somnium* to weed out any self-indulgent soppiness and meanwhile making a return to US comic books with *Jonni Future*, elegantly purging all the too-rich scientific romance and delicious *Planet Stories* cheesecake from his system in an unselfconscious paean to imaginative fantasy. He feels the goddess with him, he believes in her, of course he does, but he trained as a chemist.

*He's a Gemini, **The Lovers**, solvé or analysis and he can't let himself off the rationalist hook that easily. A King of Swords, he knows about the cutting edge of the discriminating intellect, knows about Occam and his razor. The most simple explanation for what's happening to him is obviously madness, the hypothesis requiring the least elaborate unlikelihood or extra mathematical dimensions: he's a lonely old man on a hilltop who has lost his love, his bearings, and his mind. A psychological denouement, no more sheltering in Todorov's convenient semantic stutter. No more hesitation.*

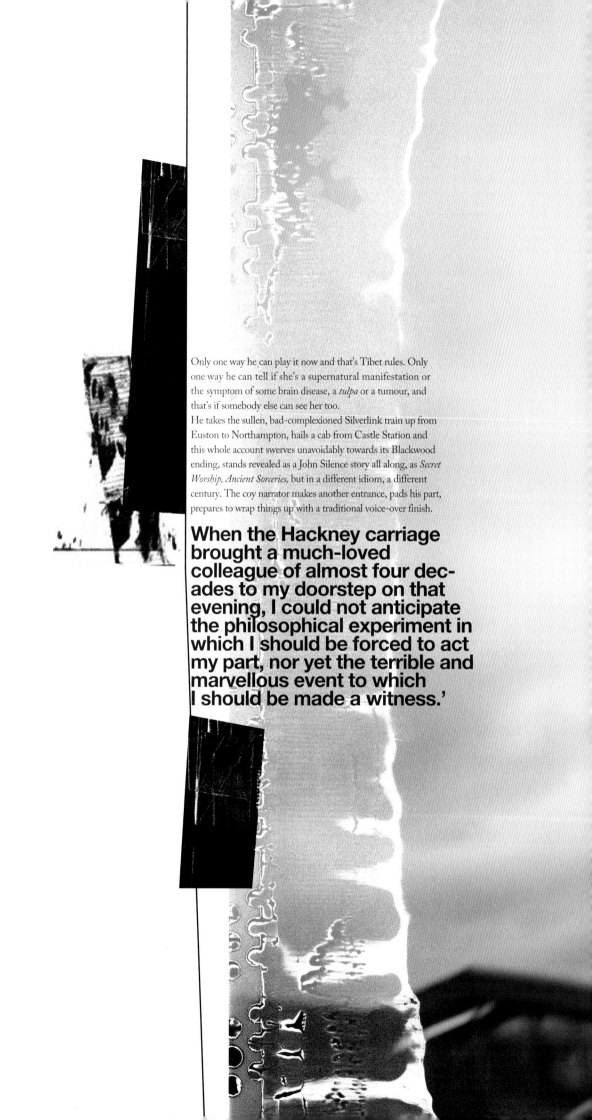

Only one way he can play it now and that's Tibet rules. Only one way he can tell if she's a supernatural manifestation or the symptom of some brain disease, a *tulpa* or a tumour, and that's if somebody else can see her too.

He takes the sullen, bad-complexioned Silverlink train up from Euston to Northampton, hails a cab from Castle Station and this whole account swerves unavoidably towards its Blackwood ending, stands revealed as a John Silence story all along, as *Secret Worship, Ancient Sorceries,* but in a different idiom, a different century. The coy narrator makes another entrance, pads his part, prepares to wrap things up with a traditional voice-over finish.

When the Hackney carriage brought a much-loved colleague of almost four decades to my doorstep on that evening, I could not anticipate the philosophical experiment in which I should be forced to act my part, nor yet the terrible and marvellous event to which I should be made a witness.'

So he's sitting upright on my sofa, leaned against its back, his arms hung limp down by his sides, and he asks if I'm ready to begin and like a twat I say yes, and he shuts his eyes

CHAIRE SELENE

O CHAIRE
SELENE.
O CHAIRE
SELENE.
OH NO.
OH YES.
OH FUCK SHE'S
BLUE,

electric ultra-violet blue on her illuminated contours, see-through in the shadows like a special-effects hologram. She's riding him, she's straddling his lap, her narrow back is turned towards me and she's nothing like her picture, nothing like the way he sees her and describes her. Skinny as a rake she looks about fifteen, looks Turkish, naked, not even a moon-crown, a stephane, there's just a narrow band around her forehead, holding back her long hair that's blue-black, not auburn, and there at the front a solitary peacock feather sticking up but curling to a crescent at its tip.

O CHAIRE SELENE. O CHAIRE SELENE. O CHAIRE SELENE.

There's a confusion where their arms are. He's got four, the two still limp there at his sides and the translucent pair raised up and circling her waist, ghostly ring-heavy fingers resting at the small of her thin back. Her arms are likewise wrapped around him, tucked beneath his raised-up phantom limbs and passing through his real ones. Her head rests on his right breast, cranes round to look back over her left shoulder at me sitting here and gaping and her eyes, her eyes, her eyes are the one thing I recognise from the framed image that he keeps beside his bed, takes with him if he's visiting.

AND INVITATION

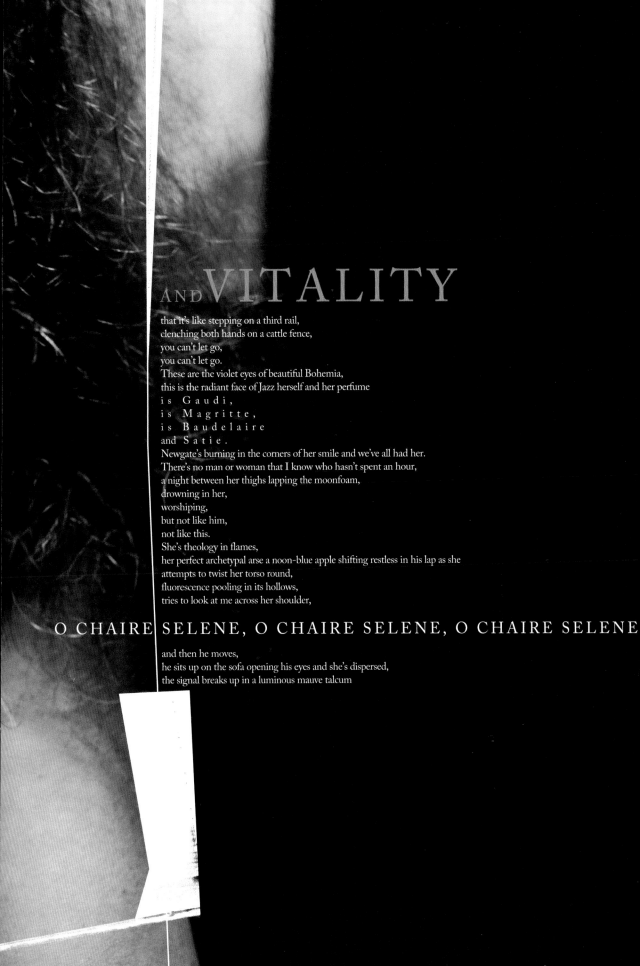

AND VITALITY

that it's like stepping on a third rail,
clenching both hands on a cattle fence,
you can't let go,
you can't let go.
These are the violet eyes of beautiful Bohemia,
this is the radiant face of Jazz herself and her perfume
is Gaudi,
is Magritte,
is Baudelaire
and Satie.
Newgate's burning in the corners of her smile and we've all had her.
There's no man or woman that I know who hasn't spent an hour,
a night between her thighs lapping the moonfoam,
drowning in her,
worshiping,
but not like him,
not like this.
She's theology in flames,
her perfect archetypal arse a noon-blue apple shifting restless in his lap as she
attempts to twist her torso round,
fluorescence pooling in its hollows,
tries to look at me across her shoulder,

O CHAIRE SELENE, O CHAIRE SELENE, O CHAIRE SELENE

and then he moves,
he sits up on the sofa opening his eyes and she's dispersed,
the signal breaks up in a luminous mauve talcum

AND   WE   LOSE   HER.

'This is no good. She keeps telling me she wants to change position.'

I could see her. She was straddling your lap and you'd got four arms, one pair up around her back and circling her waist. She'd got her head on your right shoulder. She was trying to turn it round and look back over her left shoulder at me. That was fucking unbelievable, man. Fucking awesome.'

'Yeah, that's just how we were sitting, but she wouldn't keep still, she was twisting round and looking at you. She says that she wants to get down off my lap so that she can sit facing you. Let me just put my glasses back on and get sorted.'

THE REMAINDER OF THE EVENING PASSES

in convivial,

illuminating dialogue

OR SOMETIMES

TRIALOGUE,

with funny and disarmingly
frank interjections that he
relays from the empty space beside him at one end
of the settee. Come one o'clock and they make their apologies, go off to bed while I sit up
and have another joint before retiring, give the singing violet fire a chance to drain out

from my nerve ends.

In the morning they go back to London,
slyly travelling on a single ticket,
and I've missed my opportunity for a dramatic
BLACKWOOD-MACHEN-LOVECRAFT-HODGSON
ending to the piece.

'*Reader, I shot him.*'
No such luck.

Euston Station 1 Mile

He's back on Shooters Hill completing his Selene study with a slew of comic projects looming up on the horizon, working his way through a fourth and maybe final draft of *Somnium*. Huge milky fragments of the buried hilltop citadel continue to be dug out in his dreams, hauled up from trenches by departed uncles, faecal muck wiped from the cryptic, perfect bas-reliefs. He'll soon have enough pieces to completely reconstruct the lunar palace, to impose it with his will upon the summit, a magnesium ribbon whiteness flaring over Eltham, lighting up the Progress Estate that the Lawrence killers came from in all likelihood, where once were housed canaries, female First World War munitions workers down from Woolwich Arsenal who'd been turned a brilliant yellow by the chemicals they handled. The eternal halls of Diana Regina reinstated thus, he'll walk beneath a grand triumphal archway where the relocated Bull now stands into a shining cloister, lose himself forever in the whispering ballrooms, in the library of imaginary books and that's the last that anyone shall see of him. Thin air's a possibility. His brother Chris will end up being fingered for his disappearance, what with all the homicidal cactus club connections and the sinister glass eye, an open and shut case.

He's happy. Yes, he's living in a dream but that's the deal, those are the rules, the only way that he can be with her. Re-reading Keats' original *Endymion* he notices the poet's curious additions to the myth, a woman that the virginal Endymion has an affair with who is somehow necessary to prepare him for his union with the goddess, this brief love-interest referred to only as 'the Indian'. He thinks of his Brazilian beauty at her *Qi Gong* study centre and he wonders what to make of everything. There never was a shepherd called Endymion, no dream oracle in bygone Caria known by that name. These things, they only happen once, once in a blue moon. Latmos was a metaphor to represent the traffic-flume of Shooters Hill, its oracle caves roughdraft premonitions of his bedroom with its double-glazed mouth looking out across the ancient, sparkling city. He's Endymion. That's what the 4:00 AM voice meant, October 2nd, 1976. It wasn't giving him a hint, it was identifying him. Keats' work was prophecy, a future legend channelled down the sightline linking Shooters Hill with Boxhill to the south. He's woken up to moonlight while the rest of us are still asleep, still tangled moaning in the clammy sheets of history and with vain phantoms keeping our unprofitable strife.

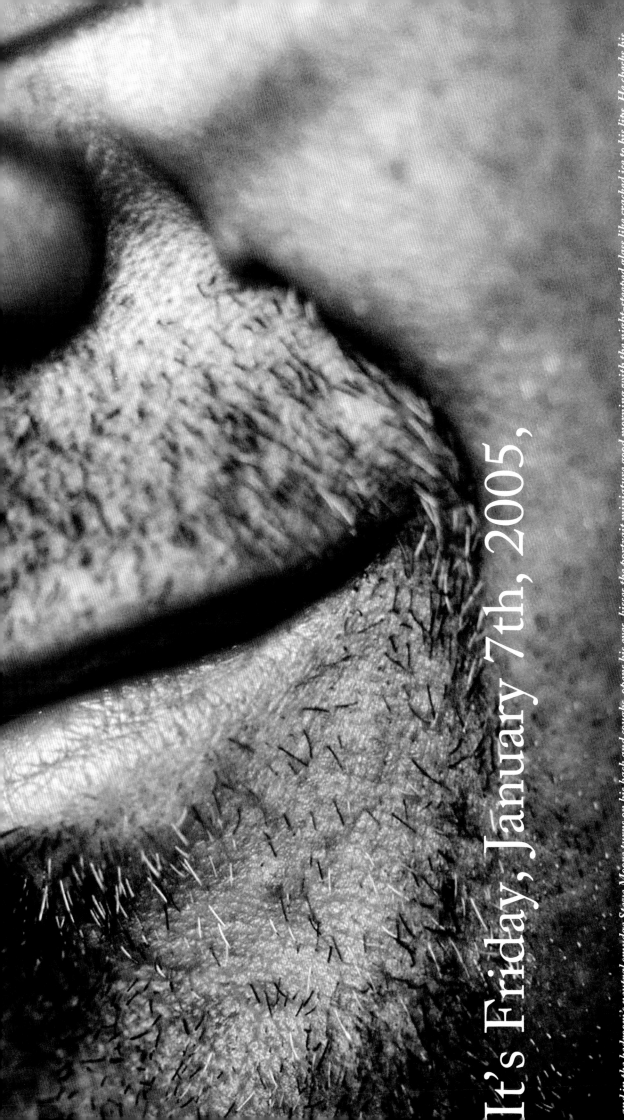

It's Friday, January 7th, 2005,

and in the bedroom's neutral smudge Steve Moore turns on his back and coughs, opens his eyes, kisses the portrait miniature good morning with the night-steeped glass like cracked ice to his lips. He checks his I Ching horoscope, the daily hexagram, this morning's being Kuan, or 'Contemplation', with its fifth line governing the week ahead. The text attached to this is 'Contemplation of my life.

The superior man is without blame.'

His breakfast is a muesli of heart pills in half a pint of decaf,

health food, over which he mumbles a few words to Chris about arrangements for the shopping or the evening meal. The morning paper when it finally arrives is still awash with details of the Indonesian earthquake, surf's up, uh-huh, uh-huh, and so he goes upstairs to check his emails, to crack open the white Post Pak envelope containing his crisp print-out copy of this manuscript. He lies back on the bed to read it with some eagerness and trepidation, it's about him after all, and mostly he enjoys it, likes the writing even though it's libellous, especially the physical descriptions where he'd previously believed himself to be a lithe Adonis in his early thirties. Some bits make him laugh, the passages concerning West-cliff and the failed Latin American relationship elicit a faint wince, and some bits weird him out, especially this paragraph. Belatedly he realises that it's the eleventh anniversary of that strange night back in the early 'nineties when the roof came off, hair of the snake that bit him. He reads on, and reckons that the next bit's taking liberties, it's cheeky and manipulative and what's worse it's cheating.

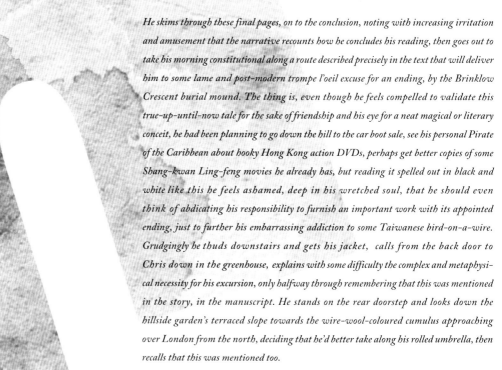

He skims through these final pages, on to the conclusion, noting with increasing irritation and amusement that the narrative recounts how he concludes his reading, then goes out to take his morning constitutional along a route described precisely in the text that will deliver him to some lame and post-modern trompe l'oeil excuse for an ending, by the Brinklow Crescent burial mound. The thing is, even though he feels compelled to validate this true-up-until-now tale for the sake of friendship and his eye for a neat magical or literary conceit, he had been planning to go down the hill to the car boot sale, see his personal Pirate of the Caribbean about hooky Hong Kong action DVDs, perhaps get better copies of some Shang-kwan Ling-feng movies he already has, but reading it spelled out in black and white like this he feels ashamed, deep in his wretched soul, that he should even think of abdicating his responsibility to furnish an important work with its appointed ending, just to further his embarrassing addiction to some Taiwanese bird-on-a-wire. Grudgingly he thuds downstairs and gets his jacket, calls from the back door to Chris down in the greenhouse, explains with some difficulty the complex and metaphysical necessity for his excursion, only halfway through remembering that this was mentioned in the story, in the manuscript. He stands on the rear doorstep and looks down the hillside garden's terraced slope towards the wire-wool-coloured cumulus approaching over London from the north, deciding that he'd better take along his rolled umbrella, then recalls that this was mentioned too.

He trudges back through kitchen, living room and hallway to step out into the sweet,

familiar

...tently, the narrative demands that he walk up the footpath onto Shooters Hill Road. As he does so, on his right he passes near the bottleneck by which the close opens to Donaldson ...d, just downhill, and thinks about the day last year when he'd glanced down towards the corner that he's crossing now from the front office window, Chris's coffin-room before ...r mum died and he moved into the big front bedroom. On the corner a blonde woman from some doors away that he knows well enough to say hello to was caught in a screaming ... fight, possibly about a parking space or something, with a black girl from just down the street, before a neighbour came outside to intervene. The incident disturbed him, a behavioural ...e that the encircling houses hadn't seen before, not in his memory. Maybe with the working class dismantled or demoted to an underclass the hill's inhabitants dimly become aware ...'re on the bottom rung now, start reacting to the pressure from above just as their social predecessors did before them. He can feel a scummy tide-line creeping up the hillside as he ...ks along the short, dark corridor of trees that leads to Watling Street. How much of this tranquillity could wash away soon, could be gone?

...Stepping out onto Shooters Hill Road opposite the grimy gateposts of the old Memorial Hospital he pauses and considers a rebellion, thinks of turning downhill to his right rather ...n up towards his left, in flat defiance of the bullying manuscript's instructions, although actually it's pretty miserable down there. The day-care faculty for psychiatric outpatients at ...old cottage hospital that's halfway down is boarded up, and at the bottom of the hill where the old gallows used to be the police station has been recently put up for sale. This is the spot ...s mentioned back in 1661: 'I rode under a man that hangs at Shooters Hill, and a filthy sight it was to see how is the flesh shrunk from his bones'. The Hanged Man symbolises a ...racted and uncomfortable initiation, Odin dangling on the tree nine nights, the lunar number, to acquire the runic wisdom of the Norns. Thinking about it, he decides to turn left ...r all and stroll towards the Bull, up

SHOOTERS, SHOOTERS', SHETERS, SHITERS, SHUTERS OR SHOTOVER HILL, OR SHOTER'S HELD, OR SHOOTERS HELLE,

this last bringing to mind his neighbours and their noisy corner punch-up, Down in Woolwich, down in Plumstead, these days there are Gangsta turf wars, drive-bys, shooters gradually reclaiming the high ground named after them. He feels a slow, insidious encroachment in the air,

...ppresses a faint shiver. Then again, it's January. Crossing Shrewsbury Lane where it joins the main road he walks on past the repositioned pub with ...etan crescent bull-horns raised up from its terracotta and a mounting block from the inn's old location further up the road cemented into place there ...' the curb but wrong way up, set on its side with risers horizontal and treads vertical. It looks as if it's there for Escher's men or rolled-up centipedes to ...mb before they cross a pavement threshold and continue down among the water-sources and sub-strata, down into the earth. A foot of topsoil, then ...yard of dark brown clay, two feet of blue clay, thirteen feet of peat, river drift gravel eighteen feet, two feet of hard blue clay, soft yellow clay and sand ...layers, one foot, and then forty feet down there's three yards that's 'hard grey sand with layers of tenacious clay of various hues, and shells', and under ...at there's dark green sand, round pebbles, Thanet sand and flint and chalk and intricately carven chunks of alabaster, the remains or germinating ...eds of Somnium. Yesod, the lunar dream-realm of the kabbalists, the Hebrew word that means 'foundation' and suggests a different, buried moon. He ...ghs and carries on past the attractive late Victorian semi with the patterned, decorative brickwork, standing where the Bull originally stood, continues on ...' the amazing and apparently Carpathian water-tower towards the Eaglesfield Road turning,

just ahead and on his left.

There on the corner, shabby and dilapidated, stands a handsome pre-war modernist/Art Deco house, Four Winds, white walled, flat-roofed, planning permission to demolish it and put up an apartment block long since applied for, probably not there much longer. Maybe this could be the house that Paul Buck's uncle lived in sixty years back. That was at this end of Eaglesfield Road, with a rumoured tunnel running from the air-raid shelter in his garden, underneath the road and into Castle Woods, another half-conjectural subsurface space. Earth movers, possibly, will find it while demolishing Four Winds but myth requires a fragile quantum state, breaks down into river drift gravel if observed, so either way it's finished, unappealingly resolved, and soon. A kind of socio-historic wind erosion, wearing all the elevation's visions, hopes and mysteries to grit then flinging them away, that's what it is. Resigned, he heads down Eaglesfield Road with the golf course where his father died and brother worked across the road upon his right, and Eaglesfield itself rising there on his left, the open parkland where sometimes he will escort the goddess so that she can see the squirrels, the surprising child-like streak in her that takes some getting used to. Eighteen months ago or more she startled him by asking for a teddy bear, a tiny one in scale with her small portrait, made him visit Hamley's to acquire a costly Hermann number suiting her specifics. Figured this for a sure sign of his decline into dementia, then found out about the handmaidens of Artemis, the bearskin costumes that they used to wear, so maybe after all there's meaning, even in this second-childhood stuff, maybe there's signal in the noise.

He passes on from Eaglesfield Road into Kinlet Road, then takes a left down Bushmoor Crescent past the current Shrewsbury House, re-sited from its previous location as the birthplace of piped coal-gas and the home of Princess Charlotte, moved to this spot and once, years back, the location of the local library. He came here as a kid to plough through E.C. Eliot's *Kemlo* series of juvenile space adventures with their wacky jacket copy.

WHAT'S THE MYSTERY OF THE MARTIAN GHOST RUN? "BAH! THERE IS NO MYSTERY. IT'S JUST A BOY'S IMAGINATION LAUGH THE CHIEFS OF SPACE SATELLITE K, ORBITING ROUND THE EARTH

THE SUBDUED AISLES WERE FULL OF STARS AND ROCKETS

At the crescent's end he turns left into Mereworth Drive, its impressively diverse variety of shrubs and hedges planted in neat border strips between the pavement and the road, a quaintness he associates with crumpets and the 1950s, fireside rugs and cumbersome spread copies of *The Eagle*. A uniquely English dreamtime that is almost now extinct, the great diverse proliferation of imaginative periodicals gone with Dan Dare and Kemlo to oblivion.

FROM THE DRIVE HE TURNS LEFT INTO PLUM

and there straight across the road is Brinklow Crescent and the grassy railed enclosure of the Bronze Age chieftain's burial mound, the skull-faced, lugworm-bearded god of Shooters Hill, the promised end of his perambulation, of the story.

Why, he wonders, with the many resonant spots on the hilltop that there are to choose from, does his character-arc finish its parabola and dive into the dirt right here? Then he remembers the instructions in the will he had drawn up, his ashes to be strewn across the mound, a final fusion with the landscape he emerged from, one more angstrom added to the hill's height, some four hundred and eleven feet, eight inches, eighty-five points, five feet one inch higher than the gold cross of St. Paul's Cathedral. When the smut and soot of him is rained into the foot of topsoil, with a bit of luck he'll filter down through the bio-degraded remnants of the furze that great Linnaeus fell upon his knees and worshipped in, 'wrapped in a golden fleece of blossoms', down through all the brown and blue and yellow layers, through the solid and unrealised blueprint bore of 1810's projected tunnel under Shooters Hill to Blackheath, deep amongst the relic cupolas and shattered eggshell moon-domes of his downside palace, of his Nonsuch.

He stands motionless upon the corner of Plum Lane and Mereworth Drive, gazing at the hillock dead across the road uneasily and wishing he were done with this, squints homewards up Plum Lane to where it joins with Shrewsbury Lane, will take him back up to the Bull, the celebrated travellers' rest of eighteenth century verse.

BAH! THERE IS NO MYSTERY. IT'S JUST A BOY'S IMAGINATION.

'AT ZHOOTER'S HILL
WE MADE A HALT;
FOR POLLY'S SADDLE WAS IN VAULT;
AND JOE WAS DRY,
AND SO WAS I,
BUT GEORGE WAS WONDROUS TESTY.
ZO WE WENT,

CHERRY,
MERRY,
INTO KENT,
INTO KENT,
WINKING,
BLINKING,

DOWN WE WENT'

An unexpected shudder ripples through him to his tingling soles and runs to ground, a horror that is startlingly physical.
He wants to go home, winking, blinking, but the manuscript contains a final pointless action that is in all probability included for no other reason than to make him look and feel ridiculous. He hesitates. Resentfully he follows his concluding orders and rotates in a half-circle with his back now turned toward the sulking lump.
He's looking at an unremarkable semi-detached home very like his own, with on the left a massive oak-tree that has overgrown the pavement, monstrous knuckled roots sunk in the tarmac put down to replace the slabs already ruptured and upturned.
He wonders what to say if anyone emerges from the house and asks him why he's standing staring at it, please don't let it be some scared old woman who mistakes him for the still-at-large South London rapist, wonders how long he's expected to remain here.
Feeling on his forehead the first splash of wet he creases it into a frown.

**Okay,
let's
freeze
the
picture
there.**

Let's formalise it as a frame description. Final panel: he stands facing us, a head and shoulders frontal close-up in the centre foreground, light precipitation forming on his spectacles, a look of mild annoyance in his eyes. In the mid-ground that's just behind him Plum Lane is a dark stripe of macadam running left to right across the picture roughly level with his shoulders, with above that a thin, pallid band of path before the railings and the dead grass of the barrow. In the upper background are first trees and then the roofs and chimneys of the houses slightly further down the slope, with over all the great reach of the brimming granite sky, its vapour masses heading south across the city and towards us.

Pay attention to his spectacles, refracted light turning the puzzled eyes beyond the lenses into abstract clots of pearl and white. Just change the point of view a little, move an inch or so to one side or the other and the optical illusion fails. He comes to bits. You realise that the glasses are in fact a pair of dormer windows set into a housetop downhill, visible through parted trees that form the edges of his face, a patch of negative space strung across the gap between them. A wood pigeon swoops down through the area that formerly appeared to be his nose, his cheek, into the dappled sideburn shadows, and his swathe of silver hair is only raincloud mustering above the shiny tiles that were his brow. The corrugating wrinkles there beside his lips, the thin moustache and sparse goatee are random stains and shadows in the grave-mound's withered overgrowth, vertical railings where there seemed to be lapels, his jacket melted into Plum Lane's damping tarmac and the whole Mae West room of his countenance disintegrates. No matter how much shifting back and forth you do, there on that dreadful corner just across the street from Brinklow Crescent, you won't find the magic spot again, won't bring him back in focus. There's nobody there, was never anybody there except a fluctuation in the visual purple, a perceptual misunderstanding, trick of moonlight.

Presently
the
view
of
London
is
erased
by
weather.
Rain
comes
clattering
down
in
bright
tin
sheets
onto
the
empty
street.

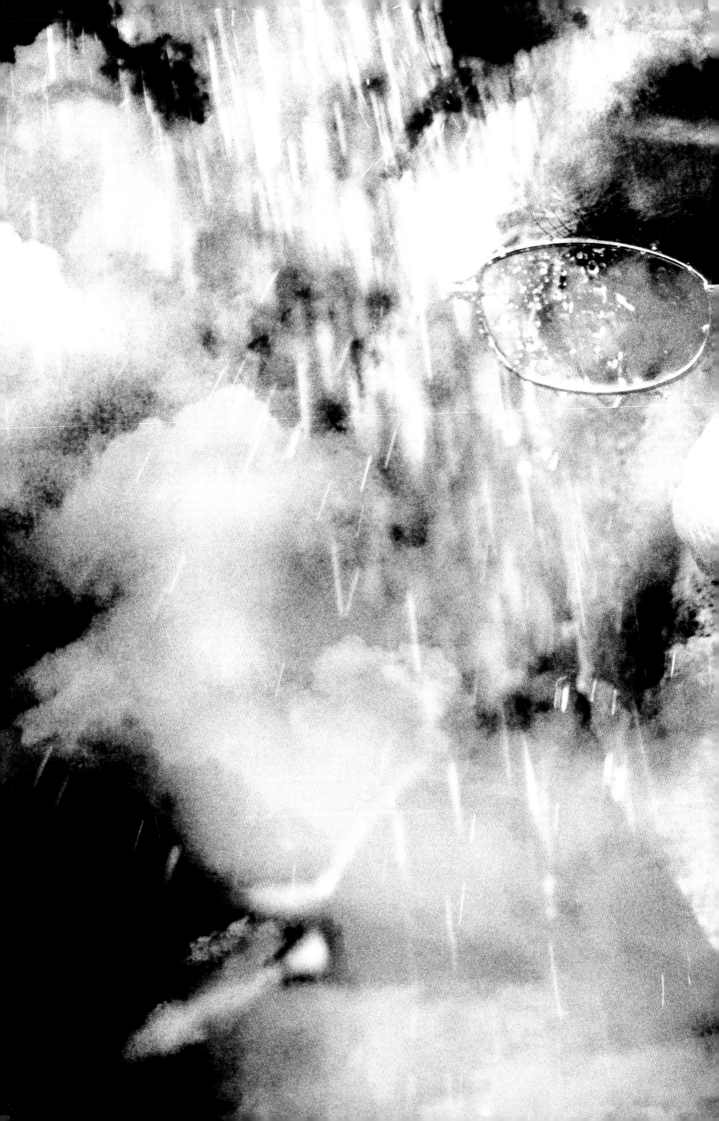

Cast of players:

Robert Goodman plays Steve Moore

Alan Moore plays himself

Coral Brazil-Mills plays the Westcliff Woman

Tim Robinson plays young Steve Moore

Phil Hall plays the Chaos Magician

Tom Oliver plays the Oiled Muscleman

Chris Moore plays himself

My mum plays Anne of Cleeves

Michael Clewer plays cut throat victim

Dez Sinclair plays Dick Turpin

Tyler Mills
Mason Mills
Lewis Gilby
Jed Jenkins are the Deep Cut Boys

Stephanie Tripp plays the Polythene Wrapped Spacegirl

Gemma Young plays Selene

Katherine Daniel plays the Brazilian

In Memory of Chris Moore

For Scarlett, Jed, Lola, Tallulah and Beverley

Unearthing first published in Iain Sinclair's *London: City of Disappearances* (2006)

Words: Alan Moore

Photography and Concept: Mitch Jenkins

Design: Mark Millington
and Paul Chessell

Swastika UFO CGI and artwork: Mark Millington

Digital Artist: Paul Norman

Special thanks to Steve Moore for allowing us to invade his life and home over three years.

Steve Hardman, Claire Pelliccia and Leo Williams for helping

make me a better photographer.

Tom and Will from Lex Records for all their enthusiasm.

Co-published by
Top Shelf Productions, PO Box 1282, Marietta, GA 30061-1282, USA.
&
Knockabout Comics, 42C Lancaster Road, London W11 1QR, United Kingdom.

Visit our online catalog at www.topshelfcomix.com and www.knockabout.com

First Printing, December 2012. Printed in Malaysia.

Softcover Edition

ISBN 978-1-60309-151-0 (USA)
ISBN 978-0-86166-182-4 (UK)

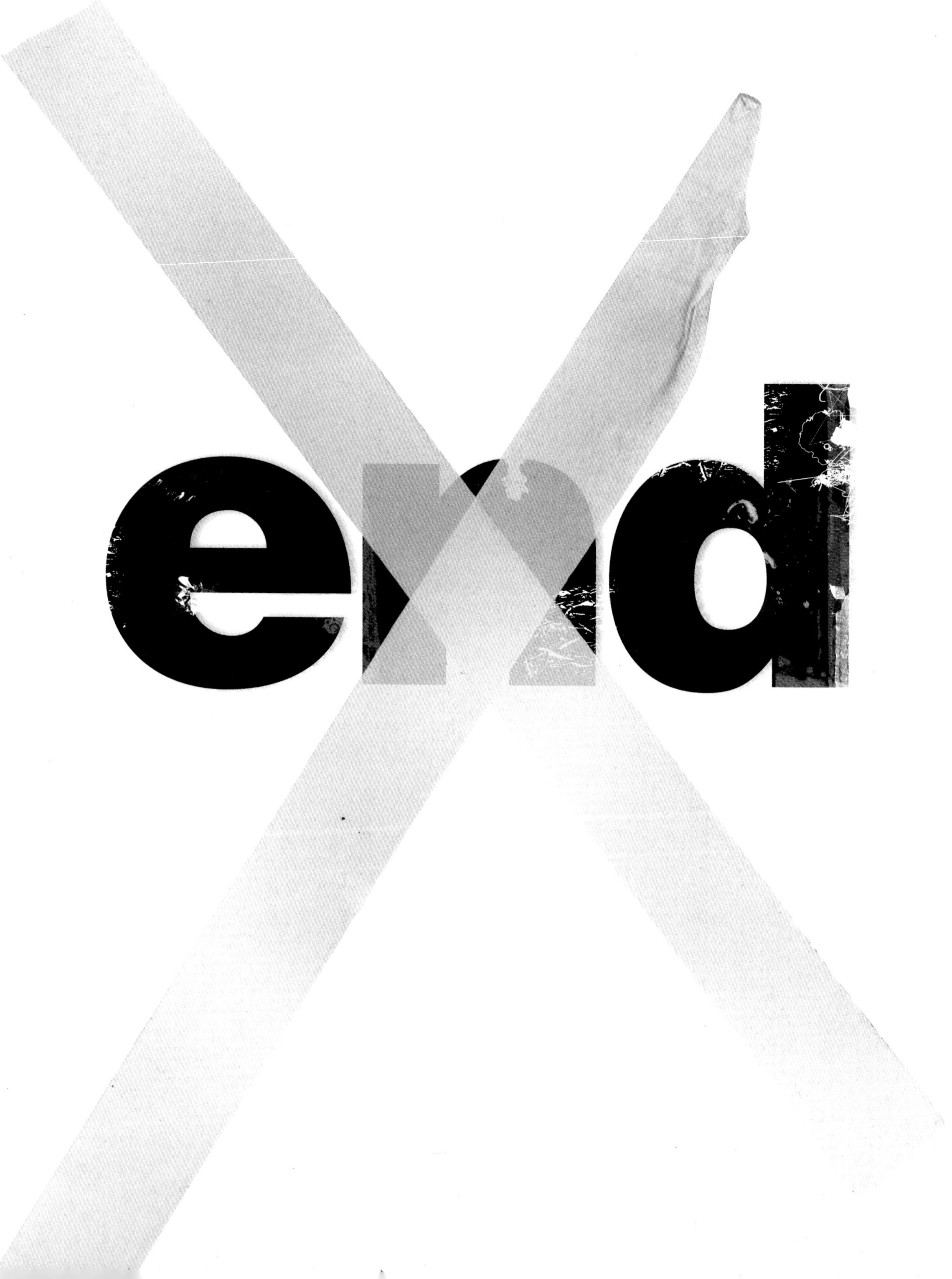
end